Scandal → Us

BILLY MOSSBERG

Scandal → *Us*
Trilogy Christian Publishers
A Wholly Owned Subsidiary of Trinity Broadcasting Network
2442 Michelle Drive
Tustin, CA 92780

For information, address Trilogy Christian Publishing
Rights Department, 2442 Michelle Drive, Tustin, CA 92780.
Trilogy Christian Publishing/ TBN and colophon are trademarks of Trinity Broadcasting Network.
For information about special discounts for bulk purchases, please contact Trilogy Christian Publishing.
Manufactured in the United States of America

10 9 8 7 6 5 4 3 2 1
Library of Congress Cataloging-in-Publication Data is available.
ISBN: 979-8-88738-792-5
ISBN: 979-8-88738-793-2

Table of Contents

Dedication

To my beautiful wife Jadxia. You are the embodiment of God's grace in my life. When I think of the grace of God, I think of how He graciously placed you in my life as my spouse. I love you.

Acknowledgments

This book would not have been possible without my friends and family that contributed toward this book. During the time I was writing *Scandal-Us*, I was in a transitionary time in my life. I was pursuing marriage with my wife, transitioning out of one ministry position, and entering a new ministry position.

Friends and family from all over the country selflessly contributed toward this book through monetary gifts, prayers, and words of encouragement. They believed that this message needed to be released to the world and now it is. Thank you all.

Last but not least, thank you to my wife for joining me in this adventure. You were such a great partner in writing this book from sacrificing quality time, coming with me to write, and doing what needed to be done at home while I was writing. You are amazing and I love you so very much.

CHAPTER ONE

"A Scandal → Us Introduction"

In 2019, I was two years out of Bible college and two years into my first full-time ministry position, and I found myself struggling with a term that is thrown around in theology a lot: "scandalous grace." If you don't know what scandalous grace is, it is this concept that when Jesus becomes Lord and savior over your life, you are gifted through the cross of Christ the unmerited favor of forgiveness for everything you have ever done and everything you ever will do. This concept goes so far that even convicted murderers like Jeffrey Dahmer, terrorists like Osama Bin Laden, and extremely depraved humans such as Adolf Hitler could receive complete forgiveness from the Father for everything they ever did no matter heinous the acts were if they were to simply surrender their lives to Christ and accept the ransom for their transgressions.

The reason I was wrestling with this concept was not

because I felt it was theologically inaccurate. I knew that Jesus died to pay off the sin debt of every person that will ever call Him Lord over their life. I believed this was true. The reason why I was wrestling with "scandalous grace" was because simply, I thought I was the exception to the rule. I thought because of the things that I had done in my life, and the things I presently was struggling with, that I could not possibly be completely forgiven. I didn't feel this way because I did some heinous sin or had a sin addiction, I just felt like grace never actually was extended to me from the hand of God.

While I was in this season, my pastor spoke to me about how in times where he needs clarification on his identity or to be reminded of the fathership of God or the love of God, he would read the entire Bible cover to cover with the filter of looking for passages that would answer these questions for him. So I went on a journey to look at every story where grace was shown, every instance where grace was mentioned, and wherever forgiveness was applied to a situation.

While reading the Bible with this filter, I couldn't help but to really focus on the life of Jesus found in the Gospels. I looked at every healing, parable, word, and action Jesus ever did throughout the first four books of the New Testament and what I found was something that answered every question mark I had with grace. *The reason why Christ's grace is scandalous is because Jesus himself is scandalous.*

Now before the world's leading theologians and pastors come after me for saying such an outlandish thing, let me expound upon this for a moment with you. The definition of scandalous is: *an action or event that is perceived as being morally or legally wrong which causes public outrage.*

Think about the most notorious scandals of all time. You probably have seen them come across your local news channel as breaking news or maybe TMZ or E! News broadcasted it all over social media. Some of these scandals might include Watergate, deflategate (for my football fans reading this), Larry Nassar's sexual abuse case, the O.J. Simpson case, the Bill Clinton and Monica Lewinsky case, 2007 Britney Spears, or the case of Harvey Weinstein.

Every single one of these scandals caused an uproar. People followed these stories as close as some people ride my bumper going down the interstate. These stories were the talk of the nation. Even the people who "live under a rock" knew about these cases. Every news channel, newspaper, and social media platform (for the newer cases) were flooded with opinion pieces and developments on these events.

Jesus, in His thirty-three years of earthly life, never sinned, broke a law, or did anything immoral. This is why He was the perfect sacrifice for the atonement of our sins. However, if you were to look at the ministry of Jesus from the point of view of a Pharisee, you would think that He was the opposite. In the perspective of a Pharisee, one would perceive Jesus as a tradition breaking black sheep of the Jewish faith. In fact, I would put my money down that they thought Jesus was a cult leader.

In the act of fulfilling laws, Jesus would not act in accordance with Jewish tradition. He went against the grain of modern-day ancient Judaism to fulfill laws so we could eventually have a new covenant through the blood of the cross, fulfilling ceremonial and judicial laws.

Crowds of thousands stalked Jesus's every move like paparazzi so they may receive healing and hear what the good teacher was going to say next, even if it went against the status quo of the teachers of the law. Jesus would eat with sinners in their own homes, call chief tax collectors a friend, touch lepers to heal them, and cast out demonic spirits from people. Jesus was so unorthodox during His three-year earthly ministry, that the best word to describe Him is the word "scandalous."

The Pharisees could never and would never copy what Jesus did and said because His ways did not gel with their view of law and tradition. Jesus was scandalous and reading the gospels from this point of view gave me one of the greatest revelations God has ever given me: *I am loved and accepted by a scandalous savior.*

Realizing and proclaiming that Jesus is a scandalous Lord changed how I approached God and how I talked to

God. Honestly speaking, most of the time when I went to the Father in prayer, I would gingerly spark a conversation with Him.

Quite frankly, I think many of us approach God in a similar way. The ideology and lie behind how gentle we approach God in prayer is because of our extremely high view of grace. We feel deep down inside that to abide in grace is nearly impossible, and therefore I am talking to a high and holy God as a guilty, sin-ridden human. How could I, of all people, talk to God? Who am I that I can talk to God like that?

This is how I felt. But then I decided to fight the lie with the truth. Hebrews 4:16 tells us *"So let us come boldly to the throne of our gracious God. There we will receive his mercy, and we will find grace to help us when we need it most."* In the Greek, the word "bold" is the word *parresia* which can be defined as: to talk freely, frankly, and without concealment; unreserved in speech.

If we put that in context, the verse translates to: *"So let us talk freely, without concealing anything to our gracious God. It is there that we will receive his mercy, and we will find grace to help us when we need it the most."* Did you ever realize that our overwhelming shame of sin which causes us to avoid God, is actually the very thing that prevents us from receiving grace? I don't know if you can relate, but there are times I've sinned at 8:00 a.m. and because I am too ashamed to go to God, I convince myself that "the devil won today, I'll try again tomorrow." Grace isn't like that, but that was how I processed grace.

Due to this very skewed view of grace, I fell down this rabbit hole of accumulating sin after sin without repentance, filled with shame and regret. Soon enough, this rabbit hole made me internally ask the question: "Have I really been saved?"

I think the most unspoken question in modern day Christianity is the question *"How do I know that I am really saved?"* It is a thought I have had, and I guarantee you have as well. This thought is actually stemmed from a doubt and a low view of our worth as a person. The doubt is that there is no way *every* sin we have committed could be paid for because (and here is the low view of worth part) why would God die to save *me?* Salvation isn't a feeling, it isn't a thought, it is an identity. Many reasons why we have such a rampant identity crisis amongst Christians today is because of our subconscious, non-acceptance of complete remission of our past sins and current struggles.

In January of 2022, my family and I attended Rock the Universe at Universal Studios in Orlando, FL. Rock the Universe is a Christian music festival that takes place inside the theme park. That year, my mom's favorite band performed, Casting Crowns. As long as I can remember, my mom's favorite band of all time is Casting Crowns, and her favorite song is the song, "Who Am I?"

Whenever my mom listens to this song, she cries. When we saw it live however, she wept. I held my mom as she wept through this song and she said to me after she composed herself, "I don't know why I cried so much." I responded, "It is because we have trouble processing that God Almighty would want to have anything to do with us."

We struggle to see that Jesus bought us at a price. Not only do we have inherent worth from being crafted in the image of God, but we also have racked up a debt through sin. To purchase each of us, that was a GINORMOUS price tag. Honestly, it was a God-size amount. This is why through his death and resurrection, Jesus (aka God) not only bought you and I back at this high price, but he also paid off all the debt we have accumulated, now and forever.

When I realized this in my heart, head, and soul, it was then that I realized my true worth, identity, and redemption and I hope it does for you as well.

My goal and reasoning for writing this book is because I want every believer and non-believer alike to see that we have a scandalous savior who provides scandalous grace that extends to all mankind, regardless of any wrongdoing we have ever committed. In this book, we are going to explore eight of the greatest scandals in the life and ministry of Jesus to see how each of these stories apply to us today. By the end of this book, I have three goals to achieve with you the reader:

1. You will receive Christ as your savior either for the first time or first time in a long time.

2. You will feel in your heart, mind, and soul the confidence of your salvation.

3. Your connection with God will grow deeper than ever.

I look forward to going on this journey alongside you.

CHAPTER TWO

"A Scandal → Us Birth"

Key verse:

"How will this be," Mary asked the angel,
"since I am still a virgin?"

Luke 1:34

The Christmas Story You Never Knew

When I was a child, I attended a quaint Baptist church about fifteen minutes away from where I lived in Connecticut. I started to attend church when I was around three years old, and the highlight of every year was the season of Christmas.

Not only was it a beautiful time of year in my small town of Lisbon, Connecticut, but at church it was the one time of year the children would put on a show for the congregation. My favorite role I ever played was "star number four" during the scene with the shepherds. You should have seen me, I wore a cardboard star costume and jumped up and down while singing "Go Tell it on the Mountain." Not to toot my own horn, but I was the best star number four that stage had ever seen.

After I gave my life to Jesus in Bible college, I read the Word of God with a fresh and new perspective. I didn't begin reading in Genesis as most have the inclination to do, I began reading the gospels: Matthew, Mark, Luke, and John. As I read these four books, I realized very quickly that the nativity story I grew up hearing in kids' church was nothing less than a watered down version of what really happened in 4 B.C.E.

Here is the real Christmas story:

Mary, a very young teenage girl, is vowed to marry her significantly older second cousin, Joseph. Already, we see this is quite a juicy story. Anyways, Mary and Joseph were engaged, which in that time in history, engagement held a much heavier weight to it than it does nowadays.

In the 21st century, we buy a multi-thousand-dollar ring and ask the girl we love to marry us. Back then, however, if a man wanted to marry a girl, the man would exchange a dowry to the father of the bride and essentially buy his wife for exchanged goods. Imagine your dad selling you off to a man double your age for a sack of flour... yikes. All kidding aside, this engagement was real, and these engagements were so set in stone that if you wanted to break the engagement, you would have to divorce your fiancé even if you hadn't walked down the aisle together yet.

In this story, Mary is a fourteen to sixteen-year-old VIRGIN. She has never had sex, especially with her fiancé. Joseph heard that Mary was impregnated by the Holy Spirit and although he had faith to believe this was true, he also knew what would happen to her if other people found out she was pregnant. She would be the outcast of society and she may even be killed for the accusation of adultery. Deuteronomy 22:20-21 states:

20 If, however, the charge is true and no proof of the young woman's virginity can be found, 21 she shall be brought to the door of her father's house and there the men of her town shall stone her to death. She has done an outrageous thing in Israel by being promiscuous while still in her father's house. You must purge the evil from among you.

Joseph was a lawful man, righteous according to the law of Moses. He could have turned his fiancé in, but he didn't. To free Mary from this death sentence, Joseph made his decision to divorce her, which essentially was getting a refund on the dowry from her father. Before Joseph pulled the trigger on this divorce though, he was met by the Lord in a dream and as a result, Joseph remained committed to his soon to be wife.

In the second chapter of Luke, Caesar ordered a decree to take a census around the Roman world and as they were on their way, Jesus was born. However, this is not where this story ends; it is only where it begins.

Herod the Great was the emperor of Rome during the birth of Jesus and his name is nothing short of ironic. Herod the Great was not great at all, he was a terrible man. Herod the Great was a homicidal freak to the point where he even murdered people in his own family because he thought they were plotting to steal the throne out from under him.

In his kingdom, Herod had these wise men that heard that a baby was just born, and this babe would be the King of the Jews. Herod, a man who would kill anyone who even thought about stealing his position of authority, gets homicidal once again. He ordered his Magi or "wise men" to go find this so-called "king of the Jews" in Bethlehem. Herod didn't send the wise men to find Jesus so he could have lunch with him. Herod wanted to kill Jesus.

The three wise men were not super generous kings from afar, and in fact, the Bible never even says there were three of them. There could have been 3 or 60 or 3,000, we don't know how many went that day, but I digress. The wise men were sent as spies for the murder of Jesus, but the wise men did not know this at the time.

While the Magi were sleeping, God tells them in a dream the intentions of Herod and instructs them to bring gifts to Jesus and not to tell Herod about the location of Jesus. The wise men did exactly what they were commanded, and they refused to tell Herod.

Just after Mary, Joseph, and their newborn son left Bethlehem to flee to Egypt in accordance with the Lord's commandment, Herod instructed his army to invade the town of Bethlehem and kill every male child under the age of two. Dozens of children were murdered in Bethlehem and the surrounding area that day in what is now called "The Massacre of the Innocents."

The word went around how the savior of the world, the king of the Jews, the Messiah was born, and in fact, one of the top leading people groups that spread this message were shepherds. Do you remember the part of the nativity story where the shepherds were told by angels that the savior of the world was born? This was a significant detail of the story. One thing many people don't know is that shepherds were notoriously known for being gossipers. Isn't it amazing that God, through the birth of His son, Jesus Christ, could replace the Shepherd's gossip with the gospel?

Anyways, the nativity story was not all cute and pretty like we paint it in our children's ministries. Jesus's birth almost caused a death sentence, almost caused a broken marriage, led to dozens of children getting murdered, and put the highest officials in Rome on alert of some new "king."

Jesus's birth in Bethlehem was scandalous, but that isn't the only birth that was regarded as scandalous in the New Testament. When we flip over to John chapter three, a Pharisee teacher named Nicodemus asks Jesus how he can go to heaven and Jesus tells him about this new kind of birth.

A Different Birth

Jesus doesn't tell Nicodemus that if he does one nice act of service a day that he will be saved. He doesn't tell Nicodemus that if he only thinks he is a good person then he will go to heaven. No, Jesus tells him something way different than that. In verse three He tells Nicodemus, *"Very truly I tell you, no one can see the kingdom of God unless they are born again."*

There are very few instances in the Bible where I have belly laughed and this story is one of those times. Nicodemus replies in the sweetest, clueless, yet most logical way possible and essentially says, *"Bro, how the heck am I supposed to crawl back inside of my mom? I am not 8 pounds 6 ounces anymore, in fact, that is how much my lunch weighed today so how is this supposed to work?"*

What he actually said was, *"How can someone be born when they are old? Surely they cannot enter a second time into their mother's womb to be born!"* (John 3:4) Tomato, tomato right?

24

Jesus replies to the Pharisee teacher and tells him that it is not by flesh, but by the Holy Spirit that one might be saved. To say it simply, the Holy Spirit will make you a new creation and in doing so, the old will go and the new will come.

Like I said earlier in this chapter, I grew up in church since the age of three. I attended a Baptist church from ages three to thirteen and then stopped attending church for one reason and one reason only: it was boring.

In December 2010, I came home from basketball practice and like every other evening, I watched the news with my parents as we ate dinner. On December 7th, a breaking news report came across all the local news channels that would change my life forever. That evening five of my classmates were involved in a fatal car accident. They hit a tree on an icy backroad near the high school at 110 miles per hour. Four of them died and one survived. One of those that passed was a long-time teammate and friend of mine named Dillon.

A few months later when I turned sixteen, I started attending a Pentecostal church which was a completely different vibe from the old Baptist church I went to. I viewed it as "fun church" and primarily went because the girl I was dating went there. (Disclaimer: To all the teenagers reading this, just because I am a rare success story of "missionary dating" doesn't mean you should do the same.)

I got baptized soon after because I was told that I was saved just for coming to the altar for prayer, but my life didn't change, nor did I change. In fact, things got way worse for me.

The tragedy I faced in 2010 affected me deeply and to this day still affects me. More and more tragic events began to pile up over the next couple of years, and then in the summer of 2012, I hit rock bottom. I fell into a deep depression and felt I had no purpose in this life. I began to cut myself, eat my emotions away, and I was suicidal. My mom, who was the whole reason I ever went to church or believed in God to begin with, encouraged me to go to a prayer service at the church I was attending at the time.

She dropped me off in her 2001 Chrysler Town and Country and I went into the empty sanctuary, alone. Nobody was in the sanctuary but there was light worship music playing in the background. I knelt down at the altar and told my heavenly Father, "God, I don't know if you hear me, but I don't have a purpose anymore. If you have one for me, let me know."

At that moment I heard a voice say to me, "You are going to be a minister of my Word." I looked around and saw I was still alone. It was then that I realized that I had heard the audible voice of God.

From that moment on, I knew I was going to be a pastor one day, yet I still felt the emptiness and the pain. I believed in God, but I didn't believe He could remove this pain from my life, so I turned to alcohol just like my friends did.

For three years I gained a silent addiction to alcohol, that is, until I had to go to Bible school. That's right, I still went to Bible college as a ministry student, unsaved, with alcohol as a vice, and 1,500 miles from home, all because of one sentence the Lord said to me.

One of the rules at the college I attended was that drugs and alcohol were prohibited on campus, which meant I had to cut my addiction cold turkey. I struggled for the entire first semester until one November night. Right before Thanksgiving break, the university held a twenty-four hour prayer meeting in the chapel. For twenty-four hours you could come in, sit on a carpet square and just pray to God while someone played acoustic worship music from the stage.

I sat down in the sanctuary in my Bud Light hat with the bottle opener on it and for the first time, I truly gave my life to Jesus. I didn't just pray a prayer, and I didn't just believe in the existence of God, I gave all my life to Him. All the pain, memories, and regrets that had built up inside, I surrendered to Jesus that night.

What you have to understand is that in John 3, Nicodemus was a Pharisee, yet had not received salvation. He spent his whole life studying scripture, following the law, and teaching it to others, yet he himself hadn't reserved a seat in heaven.

When it comes to this topic of being born again, let's compare it as Jesus did, to the actual concept of birth. There are three stages for one to be born:

1. Conception

2. Pregnancy

3. Birth

Conception is where the seed of life is planted. For us, the seed is the Word of God, the Gospel of Jesus Christ. The seed is not just the belief that God exists, it is the instances where you are able to see the power and goodness of God working and it begins to sink into your heart. The old saying is that for every one-hundred unsaved people, one will read the Bible and ninety-nine will read the Christian. The majority of the time, this seed is planted through someone's Godly life interweaving its way into another's.

Pregnancy is where the seed of life develops. For me, I went to church for thirteen years before I gave my life to Jesus. This is the process to which the seed begins to grow into the creation of true authentic belief in God. The God who can raise people from the dead, the God who can make lame men walk, the God who can make blind men see. The seed begins to grow in this process.

Lastly, the *birth* is not a physical birth. Jesus tells Nicodemus the same thing. This birth is something so similar to a birth of flesh yet vastly different. This birth is when the seed planted long ago comes to life. I went to church for thirteen years and it wasn't until I was nineteen that I accepted that Jesus could actually free me, save me, and heal me and that I could entrust every facet of my life to Him.

Jesus tells us in John 3 that in order for us to go to heaven, no longer do we have to be perfect according to the terms of the Law, but rather we must believe in Jesus and take on His perfection to receive eternal life. Jesus is putting himself above the Law, proclaiming to be the Son of God, and saying salvation is only found through him... What a scandal. Yet, it is in the truth of this scandal that we are able to receive a place in eternity with the Father.

My question to you is this: *Do you believe in God?*

Nicodemus believed in God. Nicodemus believed God existed and spent his whole life devoted to his work, yet, he still didn't have a seat reserved for him in heaven.

If you turn to Mark chapter 9, you'll see that Jesus heals a boy who was possessed by demons. The boy's father says to Jesus, "If you can heal him, heal him." Jesus replies "If I can? Anything is possible for one who believes." The boy's father replied, "I do believe, help my unbelief."

When I was going through this whole process of seeing whether or not this scandalous grace of Christ truly applied to me, I found myself in a place where I needed to reflect. The question, *"Do you believe in God?"* I had to ask myself as well. When I asked myself this question, I found that there were areas of my life I did not believe in God. I didn't believe I could fully trust God; I didn't believe God could control my life as well as I could, I did not believe that God could fully heal me from the depression and anxiety I was feeling. Ultimately, I found that as much as I believed in God and accepted Christ as my Lord and Savior, I still had areas of unbelief living inside of me.

My final question to you is this: *Do you believe Christ can wipe your slate clean through a new birth?*

On many streaming services, they fixate documentaries and docu-series on serial killers. One of the serial killers that I would say is the most well documented is Jeffrey Dahmer. Netflix released a show about Jeffrey Dahmer in 2022 and out of all the documentaries I have seen about him, it portrays the crimes of Jeffrey Dahmer as accurate as you can put on TV. This show is very horrific and graphic and honestly, I had to stop watching it after the second episode.

Now you're probably wondering, "Billy, why did you watch that?" My answer might disturb you if you lie on the religious side. A few years ago, I watched a documentary and read many articles about how Jeffrey Dahmer, arguably the most notorious serial killer in U.S history, had an authentic encounter with Jesus in jail which led to him accepting Jesus as his Lord and savior. That's right, before Jeffrey Dahmer was brutally murdered in jail, he accepted Christ into his heart and fully repented for his wrong doings.

To answer your question, the reason why I watched this docu-series was because I felt the need to see for myself how evil could someone be prior to accepting Christ as their savior and still receive scandalous grace? This is why the grace of Christ is scandalous. In the Bible, Paul titles himself as the "chief of sinners." Well, I would argue that Dahmer could give him a run for his money. Yet, Paul and Jeffrey Dahmer, notorious sinners, received sin-killing grace. This right here, not only changed my whole concept of grace, but it also revealed the religious part in me that tried to argue, "A man that evil could NEVER go to heaven."

I ask you again, *Do you believe Christ can wipe your slate clean through a new birth?*

I challenge you to ask yourself these questions and take time to reflect on them. I believe there is a place in Christianity for the practice of meditation and I believe these are key questions to meditate on before we move forward with the rest of this book. After meditating and going to our loving Father in prayer, continue to chapter three. I will see you there.

CHAPTER THREE

"A Scandal → Us Healing"

Key verse:

"You restored me to health and let me live. Surely it was for my benefit that I suffered such anguish. In your love you kept me from the pit of destruction; you have put all my sins behind your back."

Isaiah 38:16-17

In July of 2019, one of my favorite humans of all time was born, my niece Kiara. Kiara was what they call a "miracle baby." The majority of people who title their child a miracle baby typically do so because there was a complication with the child and the child survived when they shouldn't have. This wasn't the case for Kiara.

My sister Kelsey, her mother, has had this heart murmur since she was born that always seemed benign as every cardiologist told her it was. During her pregnancy, Kelsey had an echocardiogram done on her heart and they found that she did not have a murmur, she had a hole in her heart, a hole that was big enough that she needed open heart surgery.

The problem Kelsey faced was that she was pregnant and could not have an open heart surgery while with child. The doctors told her that she would need to wait until Kiara was born to have the surgery.

When it came time for Kiara to be born, they had to put my sister in the ICU to deliver because she had a high risk of cardiac arrest due to the stress that delivery would have on her heart. Kiara was born a beautiful and healthy baby; however the battle wasn't over yet. My sister still had to get open heart surgery and only a few months after giving birth, Kelsey underwent open heart surgery.

After she had healed a bit, my sister was told by the doctors that the hole in her heart was genetic, and Kiara very well could have a hole in her heart as well. If she did have a hole, she would need to have open heart surgery when she turns three years old.

They brought Kiara to get an echocardiogram done and they found she too had a hole in her heart. Kiara would have to go through open heart surgery just like my sister.

Early in 2022, Kiara went in for her pre-operation appointment where she would receive one last echocardiogram to determine the timing of the surgery. When the doctor came back from examining the results,

A Scandal → *Us Healing*

he entered the room shocked. He reported that the hole in Kiara's heart miraculously healed on its own. The doctor informed Kelsey that the type of hole Kiara had in her heart cannot heal on its own without surgery, and that this had to be a miracle from God.

In the previous chapter, we went over being born again and how it is more than just believing in the existence of God, it is believing in Him as Lord and Savior over your life. I challenged you to meditate and reflect on two questions:

1. Do you believe in God?
2. Do you believe Christ can wipe your slate clean through a new birth?

My next question to you is this: *Do you believe God can heal you?*

The Leper

In Mark 1 verses 40-45, we read of the healing of the man with leprosy. If you do not know this story, let me summarize it for you. Jesus is traveling throughout the region of Galilee and as he is doing so, a man with leprosy approaches him and asks Jesus to make him clean.

Leprosy is a category of diseases that would eat away at either your flesh or the pigment of your flesh. While the disease spread, it was contagious to anyone who touched or even came near a leper.

Leprosy was a big deal throughout the whole Bible. It was so serious that in Leviticus, there were two long chapters devoted just to leprosy, the regulations regarding it, and how to be properly cleansed of it.

One thing about leprosy you should know is that there wasn't a cure for it. It was commonly known that you could not heal from it, you could only be cleansed of it. To be cleansed of leprosy meant that once the disease finished running its course, you could be deemed "clean" by a high priest as it says in Leviticus 13:9.

In Leviticus 13:45-46, guidelines were set in place for those with leprosy. It reads:

45 "Those who suffer from a serious skin disease must tear their clothing and leave their hair uncombed. They must cover their mouth and call out, 'Unclean! Unclean!' 46 As long as the serious disease lasts, they will be ceremonially unclean. They must live in isolation in their place outside the camp.

To summarize all of this, the priest would allow the disease to spread, condemn the lepers to isolation, make them look unclean, and identify themselves to anyone who came near them as "unclean" by screaming that out as their identity.

This leper, who is dealing not only with disease, but

rejection, depression, loneliness, and an identity crisis, comes to Jesus because he heard the stories of what he did for others in Galilee. The leper was supposed to stay in isolation but came into a populated area to see if Jesus could possibly cleanse him. He came out of hiding.

The dialogue turns over to Jesus and it said he was *indignant*, or in some translations it says *compassionate*. The Greek word used here to describe what Jesus was feeling is the word "*Splagchnizomai*" which literally means to move one's bowels. The belief during this day and age was that the moving of your bowels was the origin of love and pity, which, when combined, forms compassion. (Apparently, Taco Bell will also make one compassionate. Sorry, that was gross.)

Jesus saw the brokenness, the helplessness, the pain, and hurt this man was going through. Jesus felt both love and pity for this man and knew He needed to come to the rescue. Jesus, filled with compassion, tells the leper He is willing to cleanse him. Jesus then does something scandalous: He touches the leper.

In Leviticus 5, the law states that if anyone touches human uncleanness, they have sinned and must bring a female goat or lamb for a sin offering. But if Jesus is without sin, how does this work? Didn't He just sin?

In Matthew 5:17 Jesus answers this for us by saying, "*Do not think I have come to abolish the Law or the*

Prophets; I have not come to abolish them but to fulfill them."

This means:

- When Jesus touched the leper, He didn't break the law, but fulfilled it.

- By taking the uncleanliness of the leper, Jesus also predicts how one day soon He would take our place on the cross. He would die for the penalty of our sins and bring our uncleanliness to the cross and become our ultimate sacrifice.

- Not only does Jesus cleanse the leper, but the text also says specifically that He *healed* the leper, an impossible task. A disease without a cure, Jesus heals.

- Lastly, in Mark 1:45, it says that after Jesus healed the leper, Jesus couldn't enter into a town openly but instead had to stay outside in lonely places.

Do you see it yet? Jesus went to lonely places as all lepers must do, which means, upon healing the leper, He also took the leper's place. Sin is a disease without a cure but was cured by the blood and sacrifice of Jesus. Put the two of those statements together and 2 Corinthians 5:21 makes a lot more sense: *"For our sake he made him to be sin who knew no sin, so that in him we might become the righteousness of God."*

One unclean, scandalous touch and Jesus gives us deep

insight into his mission. You might have gone through some tough times in your life. Maybe your narrative has written in it times of loss, injustice, abuse, abandonment, or addiction. Maybe you are so lost that when you look in the mirror, you see a completely different person, a stranger has taken over your body. You might feel your sin has progressed too far, you have strayed for too long, or that God could never forgive you for what you have done. This is why Jesus is so scandalous.

Come Out of Hiding

Jesus's grace is not a hall pass to go wherever you want to do whatever you want, it is a place we come back to when we realize how badly we need to depend on Christ. And this place is a no judgment zone. *There is no level of sin high enough that grace can't reach.*

So, if this is the case, then why do we keep our sin so hidden? Even looking back when the first sin ever happened, the first emotion that followed was shame and the first action that followed was to hide.

In my life, I have found myself in a place where I too remained hidden, ashamed, feeling as if my sin was too disgraceful to reveal to the King of Kings. He's royalty, right? How dare I show how dirty and unclean I am to the highest King in the existence of the cosmos?

Last chapter, I shared about my struggles with alcohol

with you. Honestly speaking, if anyone from my high school alma mater were to read this book, they would probably ask the question: *"Wait, Billy, you struggled with alcohol?"* The answer is "yes." And the reason why they wouldn't believe that statement is because I hid my struggle so well. I hid my addiction so well that the one person I told everything to, my mom, didn't even know.

My mom has been my best friend my entire life. Speaking of miracle babies, I was one. When I was in my mom's womb, she had to take medication every day because she was unable to have a child without these medications. My mom was on bed rest for three months while pregnant with me, and when she gave birth to me, not only did I have the tube wrapped around my neck, the umbilical cord was closing. The doctors said if I was born even hours later, I would've died. Oh, and guess what, I had a twin too; but unfortunately, the twin died in the womb. Imagine if there were two of me? Yikes.

My mom and I have been through a lot together; more than most mother son duos go through. My mom was in the hospital room where I cried out to Jesus for the first time. My mom was the one who brought me to the hospital when I broke my ankle playing basketball. My mom was the one who comforted me after my first breakup and watched movies with me through the late evening hours to get my mind off it. My mom was the one who listened when I was upset and hugged me when I cried. My mom and I are so close, yet I hid my struggles with alcohol and depression from her, that is, until I was in college.

I came home for winter break in my sophomore year of college and my mom said to me, "Billy, your sister told me you drank in high school, is this true?" (Kelsey, if you read this, just know that you are a snitch.) And it was at that moment I had to tell my mom about the only thing I kept hidden from her.

I told my mom everything; when I started and why I started. Then with tears in her eyes, she asked me the question I feel God has been asking many of us, *"Why did you feel like you couldn't tell me about this?"*

We believe as Christians that God is omniscient; that He knows everything past, present, and future. God knows every unclean thing you will ever say, think, or do from now until the day you die, yet He still loves you and forgives you.

In the Garden of Eden, after Adam and Eve sinned, they hid themselves and God called out, "Adam, where are you?" and Adam came out of hiding. Contrary to the open-theistic view on this interaction, I believe God knew exactly where Adam was, but He simply wanted Adam to reveal his sin and tell God what happened.

The leper in Mark 1 spent all his days with this disease, in hiding and in isolation. The only way he found healing was by coming out of hiding, showing to Jesus the very wounds that represented the shame, disgust, and pain he felt every day.

The longer we keep what needs to be healed hidden, the more rapid our sin disease runs its course. You might be reading this, and you have some things you have justified as being the "thorn in your flesh." You feel as if the deepest struggles you are facing and have faced for a time are permanent. I am going to ask you the same question I asked you in the beginning of this chapter: *Do you believe God can heal you?*

I am not asking you this question like the prosperity gospel prophets do, where the level of your faith is defined by the level of healing you experience. No, that would be insensitive. Rather, what I found as I have gone through this journey of seeking scandalous grace from a scandalous savior, is that there are no prerequisites, limitations, or transgressions too great that can prevent God from doing miraculous things in you and through you. *Miracles are not for the elect, they are for anyone who calls upon the name of Jesus.*

As we transition to the next chapter, I am going to leave you with a verse and a thought.

Verse: John 16:24 *"Ask and you will receive, and your joy will be complete."*

Thought: Can a house be cleaned if all the windows are closed, blinds are shut and the lights are off? In the same way, can you receive the healing, breakthrough, or freedom you've longed for by keeping that very thing you've struggled with for so long concealed in the dark?

Prior to advancing to chapter four, I encourage you to do the following:

1. Take time to reflect and write down what you have kept hidden and what you need healing or forgiveness from. Ask the Holy Spirit to show you things that have been hidden for so long that you can't even see them anymore.

2. Spend time praying out loud to our Father about these things. Much like Adam saying "Here I am!" this is a time for you to have your own "Here I am" moment with the Lord.

I look forward to seeing you in chapter four.

"A Scandal → Us Friendship"

Key verse:

33 Do not be misled:
"Bad company corrupts good character."
1 Corinthians 15:33 (NIV)

As a teenager, I was very heavily involved in everything. I was in student council, national honor society, theater, choir, sports, and the list just keeps going. Not only was I involved in a variety of roles, but I also had connections with nearly everyone. I wouldn't necessarily coin myself as being "popular" back then, but almost every single student and teacher in the school knew who I was because of the variety of roles I played.

Due to this high involvement I found myself in, my friend group was just as diverse. I had an interesting palette of friends that were anywhere from jocks, theater kids, to people on the debate team or fencing team.

On the weekends, I would find myself going to parties and hangouts with friends that were both very well behaved and poorly behaved; from good homes and from broken homes. To give you some context, where I am from in Connecticut, it is one of the epicenters for hard drugs such as methamphetamines and heroin. To this day, I read news articles and hear stories of old school mates of mine that are being arrested for possession and distribution of these hard drugs as well as many who have died from their addictions. Even recently, one of my old baseball and football teammates was arrested for manslaughter for accidentally exposing his father to fentanyl which ultimately ended his father's life.

This is what it was like where I lived. My mom, knowing about these problems in the area around us, knew about the harmful behaviors some families allowed within my friend groups. My mom would restrict me from hanging out with certain people or going over particular families' homes due to issues like these that were in our community.

When I would go to school or hang out with friends after school, my mom would always call me by my government name and tell me something on the lines of: *"Now William, just remember to be wise about who you surround yourself with. Because if someone is doing something wrong and you are with them, you too are guilty by association."*

I think we all have heard that term from our parents at some point: *"Guilty by association."* In law, this term is referred to as someone who is innocent, yet is associated with someone who has done wrong and is judged according to that association.

In Matthew 9 and also in Luke 5, we see this "guilty by association" accusation play out in the life and ministry of Jesus, our "scandalous savior." As we dive into this beautiful story, I want to make note of something that is both relevant to this chapter and will help you understand the Bible better.

What you'll notice is that in Matthew 9:9-14, Mark 2:14-17, and Luke 5:27-32, the authors are talking about the same story, however, they all have differences in minor details. You'll see this pattern play out through the four gospels and this is what scholars call the "synoptic gospels."

I have newer Christians and students come up to me all the time and ask me the same question, *"Pastor Billy, why does _____ have the same story as in _____?"* Funny enough, one of my students told me once that she skipped the latter three Gospels after reading Matthew because she noticed it was just the same stories she already read. I then had to explain to her what I am explaining to you.

The reason we see overlap in the Gospels is because these four books are all written from a first-hand eyewitness' perspective from Matthew, Mark, Luke, and John regarding the acts of Jesus. If you have ever watched the movie *Vantage Point*, you would understand this concept. If you haven't watched this movie yet, imagine if you and I saw the same incident occur at the same time in the same place. How we record what we saw would be the same, yet minorly different in details according to our background, personality, and perspective.

All four of the Gospel writers followed Jesus religiously, saw the same events in the same setting, and wrote down everything they saw with their own eyes; however, their vantage point makes the story minorly different in detail. This is why it is important for us to read all four gospels, not just one.

Additionally, as often as it was that all four gospel writers were present for the same highlights of Jesus's life and ministry, there were also times where all four were not there at the same time. There were also instances where only one gospel writer was there or maybe two at most.

In the story of Levi, three of the four gospels record about the tax collector. Levi would later be called "Matthew" and is in fact the author of the first gospel, Matthew. If this is all new to you, don't worry, I too had to learn this early on in my journey.

Just some background about myself, when I was in Bible college, I learned everything I could about the Bible.

Most of the time when I talk to others about my initial growth as a new believer, I coin my bachelor's degree as my discipleship. My time at Southeastern University was when I got saved, gained mentors to speak life into me, and gained a biblical basis to my faith.

In my freshman year at SEU, I took my first Bible class, New Testament Survey. Being my first ministry course, I walked into that lecture hall full of excitement and eager to learn. However, what I very quickly realized was that I was in a class with forty students who knew their Bible like the back of their hand and I couldn't even quote the most basic scriptures.

We began the class with talking about the four hundred-year intertestamental period between Malachi and Matthew and then we continued to the first gospel, Matthew. When we began talking through the book of Matthew, I grew this intrigue towards his account.

The reason why I was so fascinated by Matthew is because he writes about his own personal encounter with Jesus, which is one of the most famous conversion stories from Jesus's earthly ministry. From his first-hand vantage point, Matthew tells every detail he remembers from when Jesus called him out when he was a tax collector named Levi and the transformation into being known as a disciple of Jesus named Matthew.

If you are like me when I was beginning to study the Bible and do not know this story, no worries. We all have to start somewhere, right? So, let's dive right into it then!

To give you some background behind this amazing story, Jesus is in the middle of His ministry of healing and the calling of His disciples. One day, He is walking outside of the temple courts and passes by a tax collector named Levi.

Tax collectors in the day and time of Jesus did not operate the same way as they do today. The tax collectors weren't administering driver's licenses or registering cars, but rather, they were collecting income tax on tolls and customs, imports, exports, and from any merchant who sold goods in Israel. Typically these tax collectors, or "Publicans," would add hefty fees on top of these standardized taxes to make a profit that they would pocket. In addition, they would also add an additional amount on top of the tax as a cut to the Roman Army.

This occupation, although a wealthy line of work, came at a cost. Everyone hated tax collectors. They were like lawyers, but in the first century (no offense if you're a lawyer reading this). They were despised so much so, that even from a religious standpoint they would be deemed ceremonially unclean because of their deception and greed. The hatred towards these publicans was so intense for so long that under the Law of Moses, they could never be redeemed. Meaning, if you sign off to be a tax collector, you are now condemned to hell.

All of this to say: Tax collectors were hated by everyone, destined for an eternity of suffering without exception, and could only find happiness and belonging by their wealth and possessions. That doesn't seem like a great job to have, does it?

Going back to the story of Levi, Jesus could have kept walking. Jesus could have completely ignored this man as everyone else in his culture, community, and religion did. Yet, He didn't ignore him, He initiated conversation with him. And with this encounter, many spectators and teachers of the law were asking each other: *"Why would Jesus entertain this man who by the law could never be redeemed?"* or *"Why would Jesus engage with this man that was so indulged in his wealth that he could never see a life outside of that lifestyle?"* or this kicker of a question, *"How could a rabbi associate himself with someone like that?"*

One thing I have learned from ministry and church folk is that *a lack of orthodoxy infers opinions.* Personally, I am not your cookie cutter type of pastor. I am unorthodox and if you ask any of my past co-workers or the people I have ministered to, they would confirm that statement. But do you know why I am like this? Jesus was unorthodox too.

Jesus did not bow down to customs, regulations, or social laws, because if He did, His grace and His ministry would have been confined to a box. Jesus came to save and bring the prodigals home which meant He had to do some unorthodox things. The old adage says, "Extreme circumstances call for extreme measures."

However, what I have learned from Jesus's lack of orthodoxy is that He did so without compromising reverence for that which is holy. This is why this story impacts me so much and I pray it impacts you as well. Jesus administered an out-of-the-box grace to Levi. It was scandalous grace that made the Pharisees question Jesus's morality, position, and Rabbinic credentials.

I think the questions the Pharisees were probably thinking, we can also ask introspectively:

- Why would Jesus want anything to do with us after what we have done?

- Why would He want a relationship with us even when our desires and pleasures go against everything holy?

- Why would He want me, a human who was born into sin and for some reason can't seem to get out of it either?

These are questions I had to ask myself too. These were questions I could never bring myself to say out loud but they were a continuous resounding echo in my mind. I think it is sadly comical how the unspoken questions that bounce around in our minds are often the ones that, when left unanswered for too long, begin to deteriorate the foundation of Christ laid on our hearts. This is also why church culture, when it is formed around appearance and ingenuine spiritual stature, can create a barrier for us. This barrier then hinders us from opening up, hence concealing the thoughts we battle with.

I bet there was a thought in the mind of Levi where he felt too far gone, unworthy of saving, and seeing his possessions more valuable than him. That is when Jesus came into the picture.

Jesus walked up to the tax collector and instead of preaching to him, instead of asking him *"How can I pray for you?"* instead of debating him with theology, Jesus walks up to Levi and invites him with two words: *"Follow me."*

If you did not know already, the New Testament was written in two languages: Greek and Aramaic. In the original Greek that this book was written in, this phrase was written as one word: *"Akoloutheo"* which means *to walk with someone as if you were walking on a road.* Following Jesus didn't mean to walk behind Him as He guided you. Jesus was asking for Levi to walk alongside Him.

I've followed many people in my life (and I am not talking about social media). Whether it was on a field trip when I was a kid or a museum tour as an adult. I've also gone on walks when I have someone beside me. What I have noticed is that it is much easier to hear and speak to someone who walks with you compared to one who walks in front or behind you. What we see here is that Jesus wasn't leading Levi anywhere, He was inviting him to a conversation.

One of the most humbling experiences I have ever had in my life was when I was bringing my students to a summer camp in 2018. The speaker for the week was Pastor Craig Groeschel who is the founding and lead pastor of Life Church out of Oklahoma. Since I got saved, one of the most influential and foundational pastors I listened to was Craig Groeschel. I've read his books and I have listened to dozens of his sermons and leadership podcasts over the years.

Prior to the worship services at this camp, the pastor who was ministering for the evening would come in and answer questions and share his heart with us. This being my first ever summer camp, I had zero expectations. I sat in the conference room by myself and all of a sudden, a man sat next to me, reached out his hand, and said *"Hey, I'm Craig. What's your name?"* I felt like Ricky Bobby in Talladega Nights when he didn't know what to do with his hands during his interview.

In shock, I introduced myself and had a ten to fifteen minute conversation with this incredible man of God. In my mind, I kept asking myself, *"Who am I that I can talk to a man like Craig Groeschel? He leads a church that is 1,000 times the size of my youth group* (literally.

His church has a weekly attendance of 85,000), *who am I that he would introduce himself as "Craig" and hold a conversation with me as if we were equals?"* He didn't even call himself pastor! He just told me his regular government name and talked to me like I was a buddy of his!

In the same way, I am sure that Levi was asking himself and I am sure everyone else was also asking: *"How could a sinful man like Levi, a tax collector, be one of Jesus's equals? How could a man obsessed with deception and greed be a cohort to the messiah? There is a law written about this right?!"*

Levi knew Jesus. He saw Jesus go in and out of the temple all of the time. He saw Jesus do miracles. He heard Jesus teach. He saw Jesus flip tables. He knew Jesus was a Rabbi. So, when Jesus tells Levi to follow him, not only were the Pharisees shocked, I guarantee Levi was shocked, yet intrigued at the same time for two reasons:

Jesus preaches about and offers something worth more than all the money in the world: eternal life.

"If Jesus is calling a sinful and depraved man like me to be one of His disciples, He must see something in me that I don't see in myself."

That is the beautiful thing about the grace of Christ. When Jesus invites us to Him through the provoking of the Holy Spirit, it is not because we are just another number on the all-time salvation count. It is because of two reasons:

1. God recognizes us as His own sons and daughters and wants us to return home.

2. God sees value in us that is worth investing in that we cannot see for ourselves.

When I was in college, I had a 2004 Chevrolet Impala. This car was your typical beater car that fell apart. This car was so jank that if I hit the acceleration too hard, the entire exhaust assembly under my car would fall off on the road and I would have to chase it down and clip it back onto the underbelly of the car with wire hangers.

During the summer break going into my sophomore year of college, I earned a good amount of money working two jobs and so I brought the car to the mechanic to see how much it would be to get all the issues with the car fixed. I dropped it off in the morning time and only a couple hours later I received a call from the mechanic telling me, "Mr. Mossberg, we can do the maintenance on your car, however, the cost of repairing your vehicle would cost more than it is worth, so you should get a new vehicle."

When I was reading this story of Levi and going through my journey of trying to see how scandalous grace applied to my life, what I found was that for so long I viewed myself much like a car with a lot of damage. Life has hit us in every direction causing dents and areas in need of repair and when it gets to a certain extent, we think that the cost to fix us is more than we are worth.

This is where the grace of Christ comes into play. We are all created in the Imago Dei, the image of God; and because of this image we are crafted in, we have value beyond measure called "inherent worth." This value is similar to the analogy of taking a three pack of white t-shirts from Walmart and comparing the cost to a three pack of white t-shirts from Prada. The three pack of white shirts from Walmart costs $14, but the three pack of white t-shirts from Prada costs $895. The reason why the Prada shirts cost immeasurably more is because of the name they bear.

You and I bear the name and image of God and our worth, self-image, and identity are formed according to that name and that image. We do not need to try to find value or worth, we already have it. We just need to accept it. Similarly, Levi didn't have to place his value in his values anymore. Now he can accept the priceless value he has in Christ, redeemed by the law of grace.

In Romans 6:14, Paul tells us: *"You are not under the law, but under grace."* Additionally in Matthew 5:17, Jesus states: *"Do not think that I have come to abolish the Law or the Prophets; I have not come to abolish them but to fulfill them."*

In this portion of Jesus's ministry, he takes the most notorious type of sinner, a tax collector, and invites him to accept a grace that is completely and utterly unmerited. Jesus found the worst of the worst, the cream of the depravity crop, and led him to salvation. Maybe this is why Paul tells us in 1 Timothy 1:15-16:

15 This is a faithful saying and worthy of all acceptance, that Christ Jesus came into the world to save sinners, of whom I am chief. 16 However, for this reason I obtained mercy, that in me first Jesus Christ might show all longsuffering, as a pattern to those who are going to believe on Him for everlasting life.

Here we have the chief of sinners: Saul, and a man in the most sinful line of work: Levi, and both are offered and receive the same forgiveness and mercy of Christ. If this is true, why do we think we are any different? Maybe you're reading this, and you have nothing but shame and regret in your past. Maybe you are still living in those shameful habits or lifestyles. Or maybe you are that person that you've prayed what seems like a billion prayers, responded to altar call after altar call, and after doing all of that, your sin still hasn't gone away. And due to this, you feel as if you are unsaved or that you've lost your salvation altogether.

If you fall in one or more of those categories, let me encourage you: the scandalous grace of Christ isn't a momentary atonement; it is a continuous unraveling of the favor and love of God over your life. Scandalous grace's mathematical equation is not 1+1=2, it is 1+1=3. It doesn't make sense. God's grace doesn't calculate how we calculate. It doesn't add up how we add it up. The math of grace does not make sense to us because in our minds, we equate the grace of God as if it is Newton's third law of motion: for every action, there is an equal and opposite reaction.

When we mess up or have a pattern of messing up and falling short, our minds think that because we have transgressed, it is required for us to be hand delivered the consequence and punishment for our sin. And the reason why we do this is because we don't understand with our heart how the new covenant works.

When Jesus died, He fulfilled all ceremonial and judicial law. The punishment for our sin was death but Jesus died as our final atoning sacrifice, taking our place. When we mess up, the scandalous grace of the cross forgives all of our sins: past, present, and future. Meaning: when Paul writes in Romans 8:38-39:

38 For I am convinced that neither death nor life, neither angels nor demons, neither the present nor the future, nor any powers, 39 neither height nor depth, nor anything else in all creation, will be able to separate us from the love of God that is in Christ Jesus our Lord.

…He is telling us that the scandalous grace on your life covers *everything*.

In our story, Jesus goes to the beautiful and comfortable home of the very rich tax collector named Levi and eats with him and other sinners. The Pharisees followed and were irate asking *"Why do you eat and drink with tax-collectors and sinners?"* (Luke 5:30) Jesus responds, *"It is not the healthy who need a doctor, but the sick. But go and learn what this means: 'I desire mercy not sacrifice.' For I have not come to call the righteous, but sinners."* (Matthew 9:12-13, NIV) Scandalous.

Jesus later was titled as "Jesus, friend of sinners." Did you know Jesus is not just our savior, not just our Lord, not just God, but our friend? Jesus says in John 15:13-15

"Greater love has no one than this: to lay down one's life for one's friends. You are my friends if you do what I command. I no longer call you servants, because a servant does not know his master's business. Instead, I have called you friends..."

Jesus, the great physician, came to heal the sick. Jesus didn't come to earth to only hang out with those who believed in the same ideology as him. Jesus didn't come to earth to go to a Christian-only church. The word "sick" in the original Greek can be defined as *"someone who is miserable, spoken ill of, reviled, or immoral."* Jesus came here not to condemn, pull power moves, or have people bow to His royalty. Jesus came to earth as a man who lived in poverty His entire life to tell those who were constantly condemned, looked down upon, ridiculed, and cast away from society that there is a God who sees them, loves them, befriends them and sent His son to ultimately die for them.

God is not some pompous, tyrannical leader who wants the sinful to get what they deserve. God is a compassionate, loving, gracious savior and friend who lowered himself to our level so He could experience life as a human to understand what life is like in a world with Satan in a position of power and influence. He understands what you feel, what you think, and what you perceive, and shows you care and compassion as a beloved friend.

Jesus was not guilty by association, the guilty were deemed righteous by associating with Jesus; and the story of Levi reveals this truth to us.

As we close this chapter out, I want to point out one last observation from this powerful story:

As I mentioned earlier in this chapter, the book of Matthew is called the book of Matthew, not the book of Levi. Levi was a tax collector, dead to his sin, with his valuables determining his value. Matthew was an apostle, alive in Christ, with his value in Christ.

In order for Levi to become Matthew, he needed an identity change. He needed a new name, a new occupation, and a new lifestyle. Matthew, when finding his value and identity in Christ, rather than in his lifestyle, position, and possessions; he found a life worth living.

Maybe you've advanced to this chapter, and you've come to the realization that you too need to find your value in Jesus. Maybe you're living a life where you feel that life is not worth living anymore. Maybe you find your validation and worth in your self-image and possessions and it has caused you to take on an identity that is not aligned with who you really are.

If you fall in any of these categories, take some time to reflect and pray on these four questions:

1. How do I view myself?

2. How do I think people view me?

3. How do I view God?

4. How does God view me according to what the Bible says?

Then there are some questions I have for my church folk reading this book. I think there are some things we should ask ourselves and pray through:

1. Name three people you've hung out with or had a conversation with in the last month that are unsaved:

     _____

     _____

     _____

2. When you are around unbelievers, do you act more like Jesus or a Pharisee?

3. Jesus told us in Matthew 28:18-20 that our purpose in life was to make disciples of Christ. Who have you discipled? Do they look more like Christ now that they have followed you?

One of the goals I have for you, the reader, is that this book isn't a Saturday afternoon read by the pool, but this is a read that takes you days to weeks to finish because it challenges you and stretches your idea of grace and following Jesus. Take your time reflecting on this chapter and these questions and then move on to chapter five. I'll see you there.

"A Scandal → Us Conversation"

Key verse:

"But you will receive power when the Holy Spirit comes upon you. And you will be my witnesses, telling people about me everywhere— in Jerusalem, throughout Judea, in Samaria, and to the ends of the earth."

Acts 1:8 (NLT)

For almost a hundred years, from 1877 to the mid-1960s, a horrible and dehumanizing racial caste system in America called "Jim Crow" was in effect. If you are not well educated on what this was, let me explain it for you.

Jim Crow laws, in summary, were set in place because white people were self-perceived as God's chosen people and superior in every important way while African Americans were deemed "second class citizens" and were treated accordingly.

Jim Crow laws set the standard of how white people should be treated, how black people should be treated, how society could function with these two races cohabitating, as well as how they would interact with another.

Some of these laws are listed below:

- A black man could not offer a handshake to a white man because it implied they were equals.

- Blacks and whites couldn't eat together. They even were separated by a partition.

- Blacks were not greeted with introductory titles such as Mr. or Mrs. while it was mandatory for a white man to be introduced as so.

- Black males almost always were forbidden from interacting with white females.

- Black people had to sit in the back of transportation.

The most extreme part of Jim Crow however, was lynchings. If you don't know what lynching is, it was a public and extremely violent murder act executed by large mobs. Between 1882 and 1968, there were 4,730 lynchings performed. These lynchings were not just the act of being hung as many believe, many lynchings were much worse. In the most extreme cases, the prosecution would shoot these people dead, burn them at the stake, castrate them, beat them to death, or even rip off body parts piece by piece. For those who aren't aware, up until 2022, it was still legal to lynch people in some states.

The question arises from our country's past: *Why did the whites hate the blacks so much?* Long answer short: they were different. African Americans have different features, they bring a different culture to the table, and they have different traditions. The mono-cultured white didn't appreciate these differences at this time, so they marginalized this beautiful group of people.

The whites enslaved the blacks for hundreds of years. Then when slavery got canned, the whites still wanted power over the blacks, so they implemented Jim Crow. The part that kills me about the Jim Crow laws however is that the white men that mandated this horrible movement, professed that it was of God. Not only that, but according to documents in the Jim Crow Museum, many theologians and pastors of the time supported it, preached it, and claimed that white people were the chosen people of God. Isn't that sickening?

As a white, male, pastor, it breaks my heart to believe that someone who fits my profile could support such a heinous system. Additionally, let me just get real for a moment with you: the chosen people of God are the Israelites... people from Israel. I don't know if you have seen an Israelite before, but they are not white. And on top of that, JESUS WAS NOT WHITE! Think about this: if Jesus lived in America and lived during Jim Crow, he would have been a part of the marginalized community of the day and I would even go as far to say that because of his skin color, his scandalous regards to tradition, accompanied by his boldness, he would have been lynched by the people of that day.

You may have read this far, and you are wondering, *"What does Jim Crow have to do with the scandalous grace of Christ?"* I am getting there, so stick with me.

In the days of Jim Crow, if you were white, aka a member of "God's chosen people," and you associated with blacks in a "too friendly" or "too casual manner," you would be called (and this is the edited version) a "black people lover." If you were called this, you would then be treated like black people were and you would voluntarily join the marginalized.

In the Bible, specifically in the New Testament, there was a people group that was socially treated much like African Americans during Jim Crow. They were marginalized, perceived as second-class citizens, and the Jews avoided almost all contact with them.

One thing I think a lot of people don't realize when reading the Bible is that although the Israelites were coined as "God's chosen people," it didn't make them the best people to walk the planet. They were righteous by no means. Honestly, the Israelites were kind of dumb, really judgey, and were very fundamentalist with tradition. And the people group I speak of, who are also Israelites (aka God's chosen people) were banished and marginalized by the over-glorified Jews of this time.

These people were "The Samaritans." Maybe you have heard of the term "a good Samaritan" before which essentially means to be a helpful person to society. The reason why this term has leaked over into our daily dialect is because of the parable of the good Samaritan found in Luke 10. In the parable, this Samaritan man was the only one of the three that saw this naked, half-dead man, and showed compassion and cared for him, saving his life.

Jesus asks the Pharisees *"Which one of these three do you think was a good neighbor to the man who fell into the hands of the robbers?"* They replied, *"The one who had mercy on him."* The fact that Jesus used a Samaritan as the protagonist in this parable was baffling. Jesus was talking to Pharisees, experts of the law. Jesus was talking to people who hated Samaritans yet used a Samaritan as the good guy in the story. As you can probably tell, Jesus had an ulterior motive behind this guy being a Samaritan.

So, who were Samaritans? Why did the Jews hate them?

Let's go all the way back to 722 B.C.E. A notable event in biblical history took place called the Assyrian Exile. Prior to this event taking place, God's chosen people were split up into two areas: The Northern Kingdom (Israel) and the Southern Kingdom (Judah). The twelve tribes of Israel split up with ten tribes in the north and two in the south with a capital in each. The capital in the South was the very popular city of Jerusalem. In the Northern Kingdom, the capital was the city of Samaria.

When Assyria took over the North, the people of Israel were vastly exiled to Media, however, many were left behind in Samaria to intermarry with the Assyrians and Cushites. In the context of the day, not only was this an unforgivable crime according to Jewish tradition, it also stripped them of their racial purity.

Around 609 BCE, the Babylonian Exile happened, exiling the Southern Kingdom of Judah. However, in this exile, the people of Judah did not intermarry and preserved their racial and religious purity.

Then around 586 BCE, the Persians took over both the north and the south, inviting the exiled people of Israel and Judah back home into one united kingdom. When everyone returned though, it was quickly observed that the Samaritan people intermarried with the Assyrians and Cushites. This was the first domino.

The Samaritans, having now evolved into both a religious and ethnic people, were seen as being second class citizens, much like the African Americans were viewed during the time of Jim Crow. They were seen as being so low and sinful that the Jewish Rabbis would command that if you ate the food of the Samaritans, it would be as if you ate the flesh of a pig. Additionally, a popular Jewish prayer was *"And Lord, do not remember the Samaritans in the resurrection."*

Samaritans were hated and were deemed as the lower class very early on during the rule of the Persians. When rebuilding the temple and the city of Jerusalem in the books of Ezra and Nehemiah, the Samaritans offered help but were denied because they "lost their Jewishness" and therefore could not participate in rebuilding the house of God.

The next big event that caused distaste against the Samaritans was when King Manasseh married a Samaritan and built a rival temple in the Samaritan capital, Mount Gerizim. From this, a whole new sect of Judaism was established by the Samaritan people to which they believed some counter-Jewish beliefs. Some of their beliefs included:

- Only the first five books of the Bible were true Hebrew scripture and rejected the rest of the Old Testament.

- They incorporated pagan Assyrian traditions and superstitions.

- They believed that Mount Gerizim was the true mountain of worship.

- They changed history to fit their beliefs.

- Their worship was founded on fear, not love.

- They tampered with scripture to glorify Mount Gerizim.

- They despised Jerusalem because they believed Mount Gerizim was the most holy place in the world, not Jerusalem.

- They incorporated other gods, and Jehovah was superstitiously part of their god list.

In 128 BCE, the temple built on Mount Gerizim by King Mannaseh was burned down by the Jews, creating even more hatred between these two sects. This war between the Jews and the Samaritans continued for over four hundred years and was alive and well during the life and ministry of Jesus.

Because of this intense resentment, when traveling from Jerusalem to Galilee, Jews would take an alternative route to go around Samaria even though it would be quicker to travel through it. That leads us to the scandal of the hour: Jesus talking to the Samaritan woman at the well.

When traveling from Jerusalem to Galilee, Jesus decided to go through Samaria, not to avoid the Samaritan people. His disciples went out to go get some food and Jesus stayed to get a drink of water. Jesus doesn't go with them but rather rested at a nearby well. Around noon, a woman comes across His way to draw water for herself.

The fact that this woman was here at noon meant something to Jesus. She did not get her water late at night or early in the morning like everyone else did because she wanted to avoid people. Meaning, she probably felt ashamed of something that had spread to being public knowledge. This was the heat of the day, so this water was boiling hot. Not the best drinking water.

Jesus starts a conversation with this woman by saying in verse 7: *"Jesus said to her, 'Will you give me a drink?'"* Not only was Jesus in Samaria as a Rabbi (strike one), He was now talking to a Samaritan (strike two). It wasn't just a Samaritan He was talking to, it was a WOMAN (Strike three)!

Not only were Rabbis forbidden from talking to a Samaritan, they were even more forbidden from talking to a woman, Jew or gentile alike. Rabbis were so traditionally banned from talking to women that in ancient Israel, Rabbis were known for covering their eyes when they saw women in public and would bump into houses and walls as they went down the street, causing minor and major injuries. They couldn't even look at their siblings, mother, children, or wife in public.

And here Jesus is, a Jewish Rabbi in Samaria talking to a woman who just so happens to be a Samaritan. Here is the scandal: *Jesus befriends someone He was raised to hate.*

This story reminds me of one of my favorite movies of all-time, a movie I believe everyone 17+ should see:

73

American History X. Although rough around the edges, this movie portrays a beautiful story of a man who lived his whole life violently hating people only to leave that life behind to choose love. A quick synopsis of this movie is that there is a guy named Derek who is a Neo-Nazi and belongs to a Neo-Nazi gang. He was raised to hate people of color and people of the Jewish faith and ended up going to jail for a violent racial crime he committed.

In prison, Derek realized how twisted the belief system he grew up in was. He realized that people are people no matter what the color of their skin is. Derek befriended an African American man while behind bars, and his prejudices began to crumble.

When he left prison, Derek made it his mission to help his family and friends see that the life they were living, and their discriminating behavior was all wrong.

Jesus grew up in a time, in a religion, and had a position that required Him to hate the Samaritans and mistreat them as humans. But regardless of the ideologies that were forced upon Jesus, He chose to love someone He was raised to hate.

You could be reading this chapter and maybe you were raised in a culture or an ideology that discriminates against marginalized people because of their skin color, financial status, family dynamics, sexual orientation, or their ethnicity. What I need you to see is that whatever your bias may be, it is sinful. All people were created equal by God. We are all God's children, He loves us with the same love, and He gifts us with the same grace.

Growing up in the part of Connecticut that I grew up in, I had ideologies and biases instilled in me in a social setting. I never gave in to these beliefs, but it was something that when I moved to Florida, had to be debunked to a degree. To give you context, I grew up in a town that was approximately 99% white, no exaggeration. With a demographic like that, there was racism in my community. In school, there was discrimination against certain ethnicities, sexual orientations, and even interracial relationships. This was the culture I was raised in, the mindset that society wanted me to conform to, but I tried my absolute hardest to not take on those ideologies because I noticed it was inhumane and derived from a broken society.

I didn't leave Connecticut unscathed, however. If I can be transparent with you, there were some subconscious biases I had just from growing up in the culture I grew up in. And I didn't even consciously realize I had these biases until I moved to Florida. When I gave my life to Jesus in my freshman year, I prayed the psalm, *"Search my heart O God... see if there is any offensive way in me and lead me to the way everlasting."* I began to see the deep dark places inside of me where internally I didn't treat people as people.

I think we have all heard the famous saying, *"hate the sin, love the sinner."* I believe this is a dangerous phrase because what I found with a statement like this is that the line between the individual and the individual's sin, for many, becomes blurred. This is why the stigma is that Christians hate homosexuals, because many Churches and Christians alike have blurred the line between the person and the person's sin with the phrase, "hate the sin, love the sinner."

Therefore, there is either an overwhelming hate for the sin, which ends up hurting the person, or the person is identified as their sin. I think if we wanted to revise this evangelical statement that has caused more harm than good: it would be more effective and God-glorifying to say, *"Love the person, pray for their sin."*

I don't know what bias you may have, whether it is conscious or subconscious, but it needs to be sought out and laid at the cross today. I know there are people who are going to read this book and they have marginalized someone for whatever the reason is, and if that is you, right now is the time to reflect and repent through prayer.

The God of the Marginalized

When I was a kid, my mom had this poster on the back of her door that had every name used to describe God that was found in the Bible. There is one name that isn't in the Bible and wasn't on my mom's poster that I believe is a suitable name for Jehovah: *"The God of the Marginalized."*

Jesus's audience during his earthly ministry was primarily the marginalized. Tax collectors, lepers, the physically disabled, prostitutes, adulterers, and the demon possessed were the vast majority of the crowds that followed Jesus. Why was Jesus a magnet for the marginalized though? He was a Rabbi. He was a King. Rabbis and Kings didn't want anything with the lower class of society, right?

Well, Jesus provided three things for the marginalized: hope, healing, and a sense of belonging. The vast majority of Jesus's audience were people who were mistreated, overlooked, and cast away from society, much like the Samaritan woman at the well. And Jesus would look them in the eyes, heal them, and treat them as the beloved son or daughter that they are.

Going back to our story, we see that this Samaritan woman had five husbands and was living with a man that was not her husband yet. To many during that time, this woman would be seen as an adulterer, as a promiscuous woman, and maybe even a gold digger since divorced women didn't have money and couldn't work. Filled with shame from her past and the fact that her past was public knowledge, she was marginalized in her already marginalized community. So, in summary, she was double marginalized.

Throwing aside all sense of tradition and leaving behind his inherited biases, Jesus invites this woman to a scandalous conversation. Jesus starts out the conversation with the woman by asking her for a drink from the well since she had the materials to draw water from the deep well.

She knew he was Jewish, and she said, *"You are a Jew, and I am a Samaritan woman. How can you ask me for a drink?"* She knew that according to Jewish tradition, Jesus would be defiled if He accepted water from her, but she was also curious why He would want to drink her water or better yet, talk to her.

Jesus revealed to her that there is a living water that he could give her that is greater and more accessible than the water she had been drinking. He described how this living water would quench her thirst and give her access to eternal life.

Initially, she thought there was a nearby spring that bubbled up with "living water" but then she came to recall the prophecy that the Spirit of God gave Balaam in Numbers 24:7 (one of the five books the Samaritans accepted): *"Water will flow from their buckets; their seed will have abundant water. Their king will be greater than Agag; their kingdom will be exalted."*

Jesus, the living water, the King of Kings, now extends the gracious gift of eternal life to a woman who, for her whole life, quenched her thirst by going from relationship to relationship, man to man. Now, she has been given the opportunity to accept a water that will never leave her needing to find fulfillment and satisfaction in anyone else or anything ever again. The Living Water.

Instead of Jesus drawing water from the well, He drew the woman to drink from the well of living water. And it is there at Jacob's well, with someone He shouldn't have been talking to to begin with, where He reveals His Messiahship for the first time. That's right, a Samaritan woman was the first person to have it revealed that Jesus was the Messiah. His disciples didn't know, the Pharisees didn't know, the crowds that followed Him every day didn't even know. But an outcast, marginalized, Samaritan woman was given the news first, was saved, and became the first evangelist for the Lord and Savior Jesus Christ. Once saved, the text tells us that she brings the rest of her outcasted community to drink from the living water, Jesus, and that very community was saved that day.

Maybe you're reading this and you have been the one outcasted, overlooked, and discriminated against. Maybe much like the Samaritan woman you have a past filled with failed attempts of trying to find a sense of satisfaction and fulfillment. Maybe you have experienced hatred because of the way you look, your financial status, or some other cultural indifference. First off, let me say to you, I am so sorry you have been hurting for so long. I am sorry people have hurt you and treated you as less than.

Secondly, what I need you to see through this scandalous conversation is that no matter who you are, no matter what sins you've committed, no matter what lifestyle you have lived, no matter where you grew up, no matter what people have said about you, no matter what you look like, the God of the universe longs to have a conversation with you.

Every year I watch the NFL draft where these young eighteen to twenty-two-year-old men are introduced to the world as professional athletes. Every year I watch the draft, not to see who I am going to draft onto my fantasy football team that season, but because I love watching the live feeds of when the players get that long-awaited phone call from the head coach of their inaugural team. Family and friends crowd around the incoming star as he crowds around his phone, patiently waiting for his cellular device to ring with a call from an unknown area code.

When they pick up, the athlete, his friends, and his family celebrate after waiting patiently for that call, and when they answer it, rejoicing happens.

You may have been cast aside, you may have been overlooked, heck, you may even feel like you are invisible, and no one loves you, I want you to know, God has been calling you this whole time waiting for you to pick up so he can tell you these words:

- "I see you."
- "I know you and how you feel."
- "I love you."
- "I have a purpose behind the pain."

God longs to have a conversation with you right now. Do you find yourself having post-traumatic thoughts? Depressive episodes? Maybe you find yourself ruminating on times you were overlooked and mistreated? Those instances are your spiritual ringtone, alerting you to pick up and talk to your father who has been calling you from the other end of the telephone. Your Heavenly Father is calling you to speak love, identity, purpose, and belonging into your life.

As we close out this chapter. There are three things we have learned about God through this scandal:

1. God sees the overlooked.
2. God has no partiality. (Romans 2:11)
3. God will cross all boundaries and traditions to show you He cares for you and loves you.

Questions to ask yourself:

1. Have I had a conscious or subconscious bias against someone? If so, have I repented?
2. Has someone marginalized me? Have I truly forgiven them?

3. Have I found true satisfaction and fulfillment from Jesus or am I still trying to find it elsewhere?

What I would encourage you to do before advancing on to chapter six is to take time to worship God according to the three ways He revealed Himself to us through this story and to take time reflecting and praying through those three questions. Like I said before, this book is not designed to be a Saturday afternoon read, but rather an assist to a true spiritual encounter with Jesus.

I'll see you in chapter six.

CHAPTER SIX

"A Scandal → Us Drawing"

Key quote:

"The idea is not to live forever; it is to create something that will."

Andy Warhol

From 1961-1962, American artist Andy Warhol introduced arguably his most famous piece of art to the world, and one of the most controversial pieces in history. This art piece was none other than the Campbell's Soup Cans. In this series of paintings, there were thirty-two canvases created, one canvas for each flavor of soup produced by Campbell's at this point in time. In 2023, we would not see any controversy in someone painting soup cans, but in the 60's, there was a different feeling towards it.

Warhol painted these canvases so realistically that they seemed too clean and too much like an advertisement for the Campbell's Soup Company. Additionally, there were spoken and unspoken rules during this point in time in the art world and Warhol broke the unspoken rule that art should not be clean, but "messy." Additionally, art was forbidden to be used for the use of commercialization by this community of artists.

Despite the controversy of this piece, it helped Warhol pioneer one of the most prolific art genres in American history: Pop Art. By Warhol going against the grain of tradition and culture of his day, he became the father of one of the largest art genres of the 20th century.

A Forbidden Story

There is a story found in John 7:53-8:11 or maybe in your Bible translation it is placed after John 21:24, or maybe it isn't in your Bible at all. This story is one of the most scandalous and controversial stories in the life and ministry of Jesus. It is so scandalous in fact, that until recently, most Bible translations did not include it. This story is often called "The Woman Caught in the Act of Adultery."

Before we get into the full contents of this story, let's answer the question you are probably asking right now: "Why is this story only included in select Bible translations?"

Over the years, scholars have found that this story

was not originally in the text, but was added almost a century later around 100 AD. Its canonical validity has been questioned ever since the story was introduced for credible reasons.

When this text was first introduced as part of the canon, scholars went back and forth arguing from two viewpoints:

Viewpoint 1: Jesus's interaction and dismissal of the charges against the woman revealed His genuineness, forgiveness, and above all: His grace.

Viewpoint 2: The way to which this story is recorded by the author makes it seem to the reader as if Jesus condoned the sins that this woman committed. Meaning, this story could make people believe that Jesus condones sinfulness, which He doesn't.

This story has been a theological debacle amongst scholars since 100 AD. Even in modern day scholarly work, this story is questioned of whether or not the story of the woman caught in the act of adultery should be considered God-breathed scripture.

The Scandal

If you've never heard this story I have been referring to, let me summarize it for you:

A woman was caught sleeping with another man and

she was dragged out to the temple courts to be stoned to death for her crime/sin. The Pharisees made sure Jesus was there to witness this conviction in order to corner him with the question: *"Teacher, this woman was caught in the act of adultery. In the Law of Moses, it commands us to stone such women. Now what do you say?"*

Instead of answering them, Jesus decided to draw in the sand with his finger and replied to them: *"Let any one of you who is without sin be the first to throw a stone at her."* And all the woman's accusers dropped their stones and left.

Now let's go deeper into this story:

In the *early morning*, the Pharisees dragged this woman out of her home to the most public place around: the temple courts, to stone her. Here is something you probably never heard before: according to the Law of Moses, in order to accuse someone of adultery, an eyewitness would need to be present. If you notice, an eyewitness was not mentioned being there. What does this tell us? The Pharisees most likely stayed up all night to watch this woman have intercourse with a man who was not her husband. THE PHARISEES WERE SO DESPERATE TO CORNER JESUS, THEY WATCHED THIS WOMAN HAVE SEX TO TRY TO DISQUALIFY JESUS!

Jesus knew justice though. Jesus knew the Law better than anyone because quite frankly, if Jesus is God, that means He wrote the Law Himself. When you realize that, you realize how silly the Pharisees look trying to quiz the author about his own work.

Since Jesus is about justice, he knew in Leviticus 20:10 that the Law of Moses states that if a man and woman commit adultery, they BOTH must be put to death, not just the woman. It takes two to tango, right? The accusation the Pharisees were making was not legitimate justice and Jesus knew it.

After dragging this woman to the temple courts, which is the most public place in Jerusalem, the Pharisees asked Jesus a black or white question expecting a black or white answer: *"Are you going to obey the Law and kill her or defy the law?"* Yet, Jesus said nothing. Instead, He bent down and began writing in the sand.

This woman being judged by the Pharisees was filled with emotions such as shame, fear, regret, and embarrassment. Think about this for a second, the scripture says she was "caught in the act" and then dragged out to the most public place in Jerusalem. Do you think they let her get dressed before dragging her out to the temple courts if they caught her in the middle of the act?

So, this woman got dragged out, most likely indecent, and the text tells us that she was forced to stand in front of the large group of people that Jesus was teaching, both

Jew and gentile alike, as well as with the teachers of the law.

In each church you find, there is always a culture there. It could be a healthy culture where there is a lot of community, young families, diversity, a healthy staff dynamic, and so on. But there are also unhealthy cultures that become unhealthy because of religiosity, power, and greed. In healthy and unhealthy churches alike however, there seems to be two cultures that the big "C" church has not done a good job with. These neglected and misguided cultures are: purity culture and redemption culture.

I remember a few years ago there was a pastor I used to watch avidly. Every sermon of his I would watch because his words were life giving and piercing to my soul. I hyped this pastor up to all my friends so that they too could hear how great he was. I followed him on Instagram, listened to his podcasts, and followed him on YouTube.

Then one day a news article came across my phone that this pastor I looked up to had stepped down from leadership because he had an affair. Then I looked on social media and all the people who once supported him and commented encouraging things on his posts now were saying terrible things about him. They rejected him and ultimately canceled him.

I hear all the time Christians talking about how much they hate cancel culture yet Christians throughout history have canceled many people over the centuries. Think about it:

- The crusades killed people for not having the same religion or religious beliefs as them.

- In the Salem witch trials, Christians (Puritans) killed people if they showed the slightest bit of "witchcraft." I use quotes there because signs of being a witch during this time included: if you were a woman, if you were poor, if you have more than one female friend, or if you had a disagreement with someone. Yes, people got killed for being profiled as a witch because of those reasons.

- Many Christians contributed to and supported Jim Crow Laws as you read in the last chapter.

- And for thousands of years Christians have kicked people out of their church or church leadership for getting divorced, marrying someone of another denomination, falling into sin, or for accusations that may or may not be true.

Because our natural human inclination is to see Christianity as a religion rather than a relationship, we will view our faith as a set of rules for us to follow with the ultimate goal of getting to heaven, rather than a relationship with a gracious, loving, and merciful God.

Religion causes us to be rigid, fundamentalist, and legalistic in our ideology, pedagogy, and theology. This is why when it comes to purity culture and redemption culture, there hasn't been much effort put into figuring out how to be gracious and redemptive to those who fall short.

Specifically with purity culture, I would say we do the greatest disservice in that category as the Church. People who fall into porn addictions, fornication, homosexuality, adultery, and so forth, we cast them away as if they are a leper during the time of Jesus. This is especially prevalent in youth ministry. I've been in youth ministry for eleven years both as a student, an intern and a pastor and I've seen some horror stories when it comes to how cases of sexual sin has been handled by leadership and congregants.

I cannot tell you how many times I have heard a sermon on the topic of sex that is either very inappropriate or condemns those who have crossed that line already. My wife told me a story once about how a youth pastor taught a sermon on purity and passed a rose around the room. By the time the rose got back to him, the petals were torn off, the stem was damaged, and it looked horrible. Then he taught that the rose was once untouched and beautiful, and it made it desirable for people to have. But now that it has been passed around, no one wants the damaged rose. Imagine if you were in that room and you were no longer "pure." How ashamed would you feel? How dirty and worthless would you feel? This is how purity culture in our churches has been for the longest time.

I have seen churches kick people out for sexual sin, I have seen church leadership control and monitor people's lives for one mistake they made sexually. People will go to someone in confidence, someone they trust and can confide in, and they will confess their sin to this individual only for them to be handed a menu of religious punishment all in the name of "accountability and restoration" accompanied by their business being on the front page of conversations of people who aren't even directly involved with the said incident.

Although the woman caught in the act of adultery did indeed commit adultery, her case was dealt with unjustly by the Pharisees all for the sake of keeping the "law." Maybe you or someone you know has left the church or considered leaving because of experiencing the church's poor handling of purity culture and restoration in the name of the "law." If so, from the bottom of my heart, I am deeply sorry. As a pastor, I do my best to teach a healthy and gracious form of purity because I have experienced the hyper-religiousness of it in my own life. Heck, in my early days of ministry I too dealt with it poorly because it was how I was taught to handle those situations.

I have seen people walk away from their faith entirely because of what religious folk have to say about their sin, their sinful tendencies, or their sinful struggles. I have seen people addicted to pornography, in homosexual relationships, cheating on their spouse, or having premarital sex, get the cold shoulder on Sunday morning with people looking at them as if they have a red "A" painted on their chest. People will look at them and act around them as if they are "untouchable" or "contagious."

Honestly, I am in full-time ministry, and it even has made me want to leave Christianity altogether because simply, I love Jesus, but I truly hate religion.

Redemption

When I was in high school, my mom and I went on a trip to a theater in Hartford, CT to see the production of the play *Warhorse*. This play was about a warhorse in World War I that fought on the front lines. Toward the end of the play, the big battle scene was going on and the warhorse accidentally found himself trapped in barbed wire in what they call "no man's land."

"No man's land" was located toward the center of the battlefield, and it had a ton of traps and barbed wire. The horse was by himself, trapped in barbed wire and in need of rescue; in need of someone to cut him out and get him the care he needed. He was stuck, he had deep wounds, and he needed someone else to get him out. The crescendo of this scene came when someone found the horse and freed him from the wire.

This is what redemptive purity culture needs to be like. Sin is a trap that we cannot cut ourselves out of, we need someone else to help us. Unfortunately, no one on this earth can cut us out of our sin, but Jesus can.

Our job is to care, redeem, and love those that fall short, not kick them to the side. Ultimately, we are not supposed to be Jesus, that isn't our place. We are not the judge, the jury, the redeemer, or the restorer, we are simply the escorts leading people to find freedom in Christ. And unbeknownst to the Pharisees, they ended up being the unorthodox escorts that day.

Instead of looking at this woman in her shame and embarrassment, Jesus locked eyes with the ground, the place she was created from, and he knelt down. The Greek word used for the phrase "he knelt down" or "he stooped down" means to put yourself in a low posture. Jesus loved this woman so much and felt her pain so deeply, he knelt down to a low posture to identify with her embarrassment.

The grace of Christ is much more than favor, it is much more than remission of sin, it is a position Jesus puts himself in to relate and empathize with us in our shame, pain, and disdain. The scandal to His grace is that no matter what we have done and no matter what we may feel, the God of the Universe places himself at our level to be our Immanuel, "God with us."

Jesus knelt down to show compassion to this woman and then he began to write in the dirt. Now a lot of scholars and pastors try to be creative and guess what Jesus was drawing in the dirt and although they have some cute guesses, I will say that they are pretty much all wrong simply because they are all guesses. We don't know exactly what Jesus drew.

In the entire Bible, there are only two times you hear of God using His finger to write something: the Ten Commandments (the law of Moses or Mosaic Covenant) and this passage here in John 8.

Knowing this fact, my cute guess is this: with the stroke of His finger in the dirt, Jesus illustrated the soon fulfillment of the judicial law of Moses and with His finger, He inscribed something to symbolize the coming of the new covenant. The finger of the Father inscribed the law of Moses onto stone, but the hand of Christ engraved the law of grace on the hearts of all mankind.

So, while the Pharisees had grounds of accusation, Jesus went to the ground to reveal His scandalous grace. This grace would be the new law, the new covenant that is now engraved on those who call upon His name.

When the Pharisees kept bothering Jesus to make a choice, He told them that whoever was without sin could cast the first stone. This was a powerful moment, but a small detail in the story makes it much more powerful. In verse 9 of the text, it tells us *"At this, those who heard began to go away one at a time, the older ones first... "*

The most religious of Pharisees were those who had been ingrained in the religion and tradition the longest. The fact that the oldest ones dropped their stones and turned away first in this moment of reflection showed that his grace was so powerful that it could change the mind and heart position of even the most religious person. Jesus showed that grace was more powerful than the law. Grace is more redemptive than law. Grace cuts deeper than law.

The Dangers of Religion

When I was in college, I had a lot of classmates dive deep into theology and biblical history because quite frankly it was a fad. I love theology personally, but I do not get hung up on it because it produces little fruit. Side note, in one of my classes, I had to write a paper on my eschatological viewpoint and why I believed it in three to five pages. In my paper, I explained how I don't have a viewpoint and why I think it is useless to have a viewpoint because we all can be wrong since not even the angels know when the Son of God will return. I got an A, and they didn't. #HumbleBrag

Over my years in college, a lot of my past classmates were so indulged in the scholarly work of the Bible, it ultimately overshadowed knowing God on a personal basis. I graduated with experts of theology that knew nothing about God. They would argue tooth and nail about concepts and systems such as Open Theism, Calvinism, that the flood never happened, and that the Exodus is a myth because it can't be proven.

I remember one class specifically where I had a professor that thought I lacked intelligence because I wouldn't agree with her viewpoints such as the Exodus never happening as well as many crazy theories she had. My classmates followed suit and also viewed me in that same light except for my roommate and his girlfriend who were also in that class.

My senior graduating class had about fifty or so ministry graduates who were extremely talented and smart. Honestly, I felt inferior to them. All of us went to school to go into full-time ministry so that we could show people the grace of Christ that was shown to us. Five years later, I am one of the only people from my graduating class that is in full-time ministry still.

I say all this because you can be the greatest Bible expert in the world yet know nothing about God. You could be the greatest theologian to ever live, yet never experience the grace of Jesus Christ. This moment for these Pharisees was the first encounter with the grace of God that they probably have ever had.

The woman and Jesus remained after the teachers of the law left. Jesus stood up and found no one was left, which also meant that no one was there to condemn her for her sin. Jesus locked eyes with her for the first time and told her in verse 11 *"Neither do I condemn you. Go now and leave your life of sin."*

If we truly want people to leave their life of sin, to

be healed of their sinful desires, impulses, and struggles, grace has to be shown. Setting rules, condemning, and gossiping, will not redeem and restore, but only cut down and cast away. If you're reading this and you need that grace shown to you, go to the source. Jesus is omnipresent; meaning, since He fills all space and time, yet is not confined to it, He can simultaneously be with us, hear us, and care for us, all the while, using His power to bring the solutions we need.

My challenge to you is this: the grace you were shown, the grace that forgave your iniquities, the grace that kept no record of your wrongs, the grace that never separates you from the Father's love, the grace that gave up everything for your mess ups; we must reciprocate that same grace to others, even when they deserve no grace at all.

This is a moment for you to check your heart. Take your time before moving on to the next chapter and truly reflect on these questions in prayer and meditation:

1. How gracious am I with others?

2. On the spectrum of gracious to legalistic, where do I lie?

3. Have I had a bad experience with purity and/or redemption culture in the church?

4. What religious attitudes, reactions, and practices do I find in myself?

I will see you in chapter seven!

CHAPTER SEVEN

"A Scandal → Us Pattern"

Key verse:

"Come to me, all you who are weary and burdened, and I will give you rest."
Matthew 11:28

In 2017, I had the privilege to travel to Israel and spend ten days exploring historical sites found in the Bible. We left on Monday and came back the following Wednesday. I got to experience life-altering sites such as seeing Abraham's gate at Tel Dan, praying at the Wailing Wall, and I had the opportunity to even get baptized in the Jordan River.

Five days into our trip, we stayed in a hotel along the Sea of Galilee and right when the sun was about to set, I asked the front desk to have the gym unlocked so I could get a workout in before I went to sleep. They wouldn't let me! And the reason why they refused to let me have access

99

to the gym was because it officially was the Sabbath. When I tell you that not only did most of the hotel shut down, pretty much the entire city shut down.

The Sabbath, still to this day, is a very seriously celebrated holiday in Jewish culture. As Christians, very few of us celebrate the Sabbath, and even fewer of us celebrate it according to the Jewish tradition.

The question rises up: Why don't Christians practice the Sabbath? It is in the Ten Commandments right? The answer: Christians are not required to celebrate the Sabbath, but it is beneficial to practice. Taking a day of rest is nice and beneficial in many ways, however it is not required of us from a religious aspect because we no longer find our rest in a lawful day, but in the grace of Jesus.

Some of you reading may be like, "Well that is not theologically correct." I have one question for you: "Do you practice the Sabbath according to tradition and law?" Didn't think so.

Jesus, Our Rest

Now that we got past that, let me show you through scripture why it is true that we do not need to practice the Sabbath. In Matthew 19:16-19, a rich man came up to Jesus and asked how he could have eternal life. Jesus asked if the man kept the commandments, as in the Ten

Commandments. Jesus lists out the commandments, however, He does not mention all ten. He mentions six of them. So, what about the other four? Well, let's look at it:

The ten commandments are:

1. You shall have no other gods before me.

2. You shall not make idols.

3. You shall not take the name of the Lord in vain.

4. Keep the Sabbath day holy.

5. Honor your father and mother.

6. You shall not murder.

7. You shall not commit adultery.

8. You shall not steal.

9. You shall not bear false witness against your neighbor.

10. You shall not covet.

Jesus listed out commandments five through ten. So, what about the first four? Well contextually we find that this man was obviously a devout Jew, but also extremely wealthy, with an amount of wealth he wouldn't give up for God. Jesus knew he wouldn't. But Jesus also wanted to test how blind this man was to his own sin. So, Jesus mentioned six of the ten commandments and when He said he kept all of the commandments, it proved Jesus's foreknowledge that this man was blind to his sin.

Jesus only mentions six out of ten of the commandments, because the ones this man was blind from were: 1. You shall have no other gods before me. 2. You shall not make idols. 3. You shall not use the Lord's name in vain. The wealthy man's riches were the god before his God, they were a formed idol, and the fact that this man was a devout Jew and willingly was choosing his earthly riches over God showed that he used the Lord's name in vain. That's right, to use the Lord's name in vain doesn't just mean to yell out Jesus's name when you're angry, it means to bear the name of the Lord for wicked and worthless reasons. He was a rich Jew who wouldn't give up his God-given wealth for the God he worshiped.

That leaves just one commandment unspoken by our savior as a commandment to keep: to keep the Sabbath day holy.

Here's the thing, we all need a rest day. If you have worked out ever in your life, you have definitely heard the term "rest day." The reason why a rest day is important is because it is a day for recovery. It is a day to recuperate physically, emotionally, and spiritually.

Me personally, I celebrate a sabbath day, but it is a flexible day for me because I see a true sabbath day for me is when I can be with my wife and we do things we enjoy such as going to Disney World, trying out a new coffee shop, exploring a new town, or spending the day to get our lives organized.

Jesus himself celebrated the Sabbath, however, He also knew that what the sabbath tradition had become was just ridiculous and not edifying of God. The commandment was to keep the Sabbath day HOLY, not to keep it as a day of imprisonment. And that is exactly what it was during the time of Jesus, a day of imprisonment.

Let me explain to you what it looks like to practice the Sabbath righteously according to tradition. Here are just a few of the rules as mentioned in the Mishnah (the book of Jewish oral traditions):

- You cannot cut or tear anything. This includes trimming your fingernails, shaving, tearing paper, opening a package, and even wiping your butt with toilet paper.

- You cannot hang a picture, tend to your garden, write more than one letter, add fresh water to a vase, wash your face, paint your nails, or do your make up.

- Additionally, you cannot touch anything with electricity such as cell phones, computers, and light switches.

- Just some other random ones: if you get a package, you have to wait until the end of the sabbath to bring it inside, you can't walk more than ¾ of a mile, you cannot turn on hot water, and you cannot touch money.

These are just a few rules of the sabbath according to the Mishnah. Do you see why it seems like a prison now? Jesus knew that it was not glorifying of God to obey these traditions and call it "rest." Personally, if I was a Jew, I would see this as a very stressful day because it would take everything within me to try to not disobey Sabbath tradition.

So, to fulfill the law of the sabbath, Jesus became our rest. In so doing, we see a pattern in the gospels of seven times that Jesus broke the Sabbath according to Jewish tradition. Seven, as you may know, is the number of perfection and completion in the Bible so I find it no coincidence that Jesus broke the Sabbath tradition seven times to fulfill the Sabbath by becoming our complete and perfect rest.

In this pattern, Jesus broke the Sabbath in order to heal someone each time. And what the Jews didn't understand was that although Jesus was breaking their tradition of what "rest" looked like, the biblical definition of "rest" actually means to have "patient expectation." The people that Jesus healed had a patient expectation of being healed of their ailments and disabilities. And it was through those instances of healing that Jesus brought true rest to those he healed. Jesus became the embodiment of rest. This is why He instructs in Matthew 11, *"Come to me all who are weary and burdened, and I will give you rest."*

My Personal Journey with Rest

Personally, I love this word *"anapauo"* which is the biblical word for rest. As I just mentioned, this word means "patient expectation." In Hebrew, the word primarily used for rest is the word "shabbat" which means "to sit still."

In 2021, the Lord challenged me with a verse found in Psalms 46:10 which says, *"Be still and know that I am God."* What the Lord showed me was this connection between the Greek word for rest, the Hebrew word for rest, and the Hebrew word for being "still" as seen in this passage. The word "still" found in Psalms 46:10 is the Hebrew word *"rapa"* which is defined as "to let down your hands" or as I like to define it: *"As I lay my hands down, God extends His."* And it was then that I realized that all my efforts and striving were nothing compared to what the miraculous hands of God can do.

The reason why He challenged me with this verse is because I was in an extremely difficult season in my life. In 2020, I went through a divorce and it was a difficult time for me. I was dealing with abandonment issues, loneliness, and as helpful as therapy was, it showed me things in myself I never saw, and it was hard for me to accept.

The day my divorce was filed, I went and hung out with my best friends, Ray and Ethan. On our way to Waffle House, Ethan told me about how his mom heard from God about the situation I was in, and his mom was given a word from God to tell me, and that word was to not worry because "another is on the way" and she described the woman I would eventually be married to. Two days later, my friend Jackie came to my office, and she told me the Lord told her to give a message to me and it was the same that Ethan's mom had for me.

Because of the loneliness, emotional instability, and trauma I experienced, in my mind, I began trying to identify and cram women into this mold of the description of this woman that God allegedly created for me. I was trying in my own knowledge to figure out who this mystery woman was. I was asking myself questions like: *"Who is this woman that is supposed to partner with me in ministry? Who is this woman that is supposed to be the mother of my children? Who is she?"* My mind just kept trying to figure out who this woman could be, and my efforts led me nowhere except in a place of frantic expectation, not patient expectation.

Then one day in my personal time with Jesus, He encouraged me with that verse: *"Be still and know I am God."* Here I found myself in patient expectation (*anapauo*), to be still (*shabat*), and let God do what he promised and for me not to interfere with that plan (*rapa*).

A few months later, a woman showed up to my church's small group and I thought she was pretty dang gorgeous. But I remembered what God told me, *"Be still."* (Also, low-key I was intimidated by her because she always came to small group in her nursing scrubs after a twelve- hour shift and it looked like she had her whole life together because she was an independent, successful woman.)

This woman was an esteemed nurse who specialized in high-risk OB. She always came to group after working a laboring twelve-hour shift at a hospital over an hour away. Every time she spoke, she talked with such great maturity. And then there was me who was this emotionally damaged dude who just went through a pretty traumatic experience. So, my thought was, *This girl is way out of my league.*

Then on Halloween of that year, I felt the Lord tell me in my apartment to start praying for my future wife and for two hours I paced my apartment praying for this mystery woman. A few weeks later, the Lord gave me the eyes to see that this mystery woman had been right in front of me this whole time, and I had no idea. It was the woman who had been attending my small group for the past month. I knew then it was time to pursue her, and I did. And as I found out her story, it only brought more and more confirmation that this was the woman I was supposed to be with the whole time.

On December 22, 2022, we got married and we themed our wedding not just with a color palette, but we themed it: the faithfulness of God. God was faithful to heal me. His grace and His favor showed that He wasn't done with me yet, He showed that He knew me, He knew my needs, my desires, and hey, He knew my type too ;). YOU GO, GOD!

Patient expectation through the act of laying our hands down for God to extend His, that is true rest. And what we find in each of the seven stories of Jesus healing on the Sabbath, someone that had patient expectations received the grace and healing of Christ.

The Seven Healings

So where can these seven healings be found in scripture? Here's the list:

1. Jesus heals a man with an unclean spirit (Mark 1:21-28; Luke 4:31-36)

2. Jesus heals Peter's mom-in-law (Matthew 8:14-15; Mark 1:29-31; Luke 4:38-39)

3. Jesus heals a man with a withered hand (Matthew 12:9-13; Mark 3:1-6; Luke 6:6-11)

4. Jesus heals a disabled man (John 5:1-17)

5. Jesus heals a blind man (John 9:1-12)

6. Jesus heals a disabled woman (Luke 13:10-17)

7. Jesus heals a man with swelling of the flesh (Luke 14:1-6)

What you notice as an underlying theme is that in many of these stories, the people with these ailments had them for a long time. The man with the withered hand had a progressive form of paralysis that happened over the years, the disabled man had been in that condition for thirty-eight years, the blind man was blind from birth, and the disabled woman had been like that for eighteen years.

The universal theme amongst all seven of those that were healed was that they had a patient expectation that Jesus, the man they call "the Christ," could bring them healing. And He did.

Now you've read this far and you're probably wondering "where is the scandal?" Here is the scandal: Jesus not only broke the Sabbath, he intentionally did it in front of the teachers and enforcers of the law, and the law states in Exodus 35:2, *"For six days, work is to be done, but the seventh day shall be your holy day, a day of sabbath rest to the Lord. Whoever does any work on it is to be put to death."*

Here is the scandal: the cost for Jesus to heal these people on the sabbath, according to the tradition of the law, was death. And in the same way, in order for Christ to extend His hands in our patient expectation, He faced a death where His hands were extended and pierced in order for us to find His grace.

Jesus broke a tradition that was punishable by death to heal people with long suffering. The fact is that whatever long suffering you have been experiencing, Jesus is willing to break all tradition to get to you.

In the story of the prodigal son, Jesus described how the son who ran away with his inheritance splurged it on temporary doses of happiness and dopamine. When he ran out of money though, he lived with the pigs, ate what they ate, and experienced suffering. It was then that he realized that he could just go home to his father. On his way back, his father was waiting for his son to return. His father had patient expectation that his son would come back home.

When his father saw his son from far away, Jesus says that the father began to run toward his son. This broke tradition. This wealthy man had to gird his loins, most likely exposing himself while running to his son. The father didn't care about tradition at that moment. His son was coming home and his compassion for his son overwhelmed him to the point that he would break any tradition to get to him and show him grace and love.

Jesus has so much compassion for you and me that he broke traditions to show us grace and ultimately died for our sake. Do you comprehend the grace of Christ yet? We are seven chapters into this, and I guarantee there are some of you reading this right now and you still aren't able to truly comprehend the grace that Jesus has for you, the individual.

Jesus crossed all borders of tradition regardless of the consequences just to get to you, heal you, and pardon you of your sin. His grace is so scandalous that He is willing to fulfill law, break tradition, go homeless, endure unbearable suffering, and ultimately die just to save you from enduring an eternity without him.

The God who loves you, cherishes you, and forgives you no matter where you go or what you do sent His son to live a life blameless so you would be as well. Really think about that. Let it sink in.

The pattern of Jesus's grace can overcome any pattern of sin you may be stuck in. And in your patient expectation, Jesus says in 2 Corinthians 12:9, *"My grace is sufficient for you, for my power is made perfect in weakness."*

Whatever weakness, deficiency, or disability you are experiencing currently in your life, Jesus's grace extends to you. In your patient expectation, the power of God is deemed perfect to move in your weakness, deficiency, or disability.

As we move on to chapter eight, ask yourself these questions:

1. What am I patiently expecting in my life?

2. Do I find rest in Jesus?

3. What is an area of my life that I need the grace and power of God to move in?

I'll see you in chapter eight!

"A Scandal → Us Sight"

Key quote:

"It is better to take refuge in the Lord than to trust in humans. It is better to take refuge in the Lord than to trust in princes."

Psalms 118:8-9

Last year, a very famous pastor was under a lot of scrutiny for a sermon illustration of his. This pastor called up a volunteer and preached a sermon on the blind man who was healed by Jesus.

In this story, Jesus saw a man who was blind since birth, spit on the ground to make mud, rubbed the mud on the eyes of this blind man, and after washing them in the pools of Siloam, VOILA! He was healed.

Now this pastor I am speaking of proceeded to spit into his hand and make obscene noises of getting the phlegm out of his throat. He swished the spit around in his cupped hand and stirred it with his finger. He proceeded to spread the ounce of spit onto the face of this volunteer. Pretty scandalous right?

Well, what if I told you that although this is a very gross illustration to us, in the day and time of Jesus, it actually wasn't. I know, spit is spit. It is nasty. But what if I told you that in the day and age of Jesus, spit actually was believed to have distinct healing properties?

In fact, three times in the gospels we read of Jesus healing someone with his spit. In Mark chapter 7, a man is given to Jesus who was deaf and could barely talk. Jesus pulled the man aside, put his fingers in the man's ears, spit on his fingers, and touched the man's tongue. The man began speaking normally and could hear.

Then in Mark chapter 8, a blind man in Bethsaida begged to touch Jesus because he knew a touch from Jesus could heal his blindness. Jesus took the blind man outside the village, spit on the man's eyes and placed His hands on him twice, and his sight was restored.

Then we find ourselves here in John chapter 9, the third time that Jesus has healed someone with spit, but this time, making mud with His spit, He heals the blind man.

What's Up with All of This Spit?

In our culture, to spit on someone is seen as one of the greatest forms of disrespect. I remember when I was in Jerusalem, I was walking on the streets with some of my friends and a Hasidic Jewish man spit in my direction because I said to my friends that Jesus is the Messiah. He knew if he spit at me, it would show to me that he doesn't respect me.

With Jesus however, the message seems to be completely different because in the culture of His time, the ideology of saliva had an opposite connotation. When Jesus was doing His earthly ministry, there were a few beliefs with saliva:

1. Saliva could be used as a medicine.

2. Saliva from a distinguished person had curative properties.

3. Saliva, at times, was seen as the equivalent of anointing oil.

This wasn't just an old wives tale though, this was a legitimately documented theory. Writers such as the renowned Pliny wrote about how people would use saliva, especially that of distinguished people, for medicinal use. One writer once documented how Emperor Vespasian, who reigned just before the birth of Christ, spit into a man's eyes much like Jesus did and for the same purpose as Jesus did: to heal him.

Saliva was used as a safeguard against snakes, it was used to cure pink eye, and if you spit three times before taking medicine, it was believed to increase the effectiveness of the medicine. Additionally, the use of "fasted saliva" was great. This saliva was harvested while someone was fasting, typically right after waking up. Fasting saliva was used to cure all sorts of inflammation including sore necks and it could even kill venomous creatures.

The fact that Jesus used His spit on this man in John chapter nine, during this day and age, was not that uncommon or weird. But it was scandalous. Out of the three times that Jesus healed someone with His spit, our story in John 9 is the only time that Jesus didn't lead the individual to a place of privacy. He did it out in the open for everyone to see, even the Pharisees.

Using spit on this man was pretty scandalous, but the story gets even juicier. In verse 6 we read that Jesus made mud with His spit. In Greek, the word used for mud here is actually *pelos* which means "clay that is used for pottery."

Where else have we seen clay and pottery in the Bible? Well one of the most well-known verses using these two words is found in Isaiah 64:8 which reads, *"Yet you, Lord, are our Father. We are the clay, you are the potter; we are all the work of your hand."*

This man had been blind since birth. A work of the hands of God now had a broken piece. So, Jesus knew that in order to fix the broken piece of this work of God was to create clay once again and restore the sight of the blind man.

Jesus spit on the ground and created clay, the kind a potter would use according to the Greek definition, and He rubbed it on the eyes of the blind man. This is where the scandal starts cooking. Jesus didn't just use His spit to heal a man in public, Jesus created clay with His spit and rubbed it on this man's eyes. On top of all of this, He did it on the Sabbath.

In the previous chapter we talked through the "Scandal-Us Pattern" of Jesus and how Jesus healed people seven times on the Sabbath, disregarding the traditions of this once sacred day. This story in John 9 is one of those seven instances.

Scandalous Mud

Once Jesus made the clay, this is where the scandal began to rise. According to Shabbat 108:20 in the Mishnah, it states *"To heal a blind man on the Sabbath is prohibited... it is also prohibited to make mud with spittle and smear it on his eyes."* As I mentioned in the last chapter, the cost of disobeying the statues of the Sabbath was the penalty of death.

Jesus faced the potential of being killed for restoring the man's sight. And as we continue in the story, we notice something unusual. After Jesus rubs the clay on the man's eyes and tells the man to wash off in the pool of Siloam, Jesus disappears in the narrative for a bit. Meaning, Jesus only had a part in this scandal, the person the scandal really revolved around was the blind man.

So, let's explore the rest of this story from the man's perspective. Just for clarity's sake, let's call the blind man "Joe."

Joe walks with clay in his eyes to the pools of Siloam. This pool was the only freshwater source in Jerusalem during this time. During the feast of tabernacles, they would draw water from this pool in order to fulfill the scripture in Isaiah 12:3, *"With joy you will draw water from the wells of salvation."*

Joe, with clay in his eyes made from the dirt he was created from and the spit of his savior, cleanses his eyes in the pool. While in the Pool of Siloam, as Joe's sight was restored, he was restored in the sight of his heavenly Father and cleansed of his sin.

Joe walks back home and immediately the neighbors who saw him on the side of the street begging for food and change over the years, see him healed of his disability. They are amazed, yet curious, and doubtful, all at the same time. They start asking questions and then to confirm this was real, they brought along the Pharisees to see what had happened and judge for themselves the validity of this healing.

The Pharisees begin interrogating Joe of his now past disability, the validity of it, and the encounter he had with Jesus. Joe admits that Jesus is a prophet, that He has divine healing power, and that He had to be of God or else He couldn't have done this kind of healing.

Now during this point in Jesus's ministry, if someone confessed Jesus as the Christ, they would be banished and excommunicated from the synagogue to the point that if they continued to profess Christ, they would be treated in society as a leper.

Joe didn't care, but his parents did. The Pharisees asked them all about what had happened, and they deflected their answer to force their son to answer so they wouldn't be excommunicated.

The Pharisees summoned Joe once again and they treated him terribly. They insulted him, emotionally abused him, and then they excommunicated him. But he left unphased. The scripture didn't say he was sad or anything like that.

In Matthew 12, Jesus calls the Pharisees a brood of vipers; and if we go back to the very beginning of this chapter, we see that saliva was used as a deterrent against venomous creatures including snakes. In addition, when "Joe" was telling his neighbors about what Jesus did, he said *"The man called Jesus made mud and anointed my eyes."*

The most famous scripture about "anointing" in the Bible is found in Psalms 23 where David writes in the perspective of him being a sheep and the Lord being his shepherd. He lists all the acts of service his shepherd does for him and in verse 5, he writes *"You prepare a table before me in the presence of my enemies. You anoint my head with oil; my cup overflows."*

The anointing oil David speaks of here isn't the oil that Pentecostal preachers lather onto the foreheads of their congregants for the sake of deliverance. This oil was placed on the head of the sheep as a deterrent from their prey, or "enemies."

Sheep had three types of predators at this time: flies, wolves, and snakes. In this passage, David says that the Lord placed him in front of his enemies, yet he remained unharmed because he had the anointing oil of his shepherd on him as a protectant.

The spit, or "anointing oil" of Jesus acted as a protectant for the blind man against the Pharisees (AKA Brood of Vipers) who for decades would scour at him, look down upon him, and look at him with disgust because they thought his "sin" was what made him blind. Regardless of being insulted, emotionally abused, and excommunicated, he left unphased, only to be delivered into the hands of Jesus who would welcome him with open arms.

I know I've talked a lot about the story and historic background of this passage in this chapter, but the reason why is because I needed to paint the picture for you of what this man felt before Jesus and how he felt after Jesus.

Every chapter thus far, and going forward, I have highlighted a specific person that each chapter and scandal speaks to. This chapter is for those who have been hurt by religious people.

I want you to notice that I did not say "those with church hurt." Personally, I do not like the term "church hurt." I say this not to discredit your experiences or feelings, I say this because the church is not what is flawed, it is the people. If the bride of Christ is the bride of Christ, it is perfect. But the people who make up the bride are imperfect and flawed.

So, for those with "church hurt," your pain is at the hand of religious people. Religious people are those who use their position, in conjunction with an eisegetical view of the word of God, for personal gain, power, or to commit abuse. Religious people are those that use fundamentalism and legalism to create their own set of rules outside of the word of God to strictly enforce their ideologies.

When I think of religious people, I think of the people with megaphones and picket signs at big events that tell people they're going to hell. I think of people that excommunicate people from their "church" because they didn't agree with their theology, ideologies, or other various statutes. I think of people who really believe that if sinners go to church, that those sinners will be struck by lightning once they enter into the church. I think of people who use skewed Christian values and concepts for their own gain. I think of people who, because the Bible says something is a sin, will spew hatred toward those whose struggles fall into that sin category.

I will never forget when I was in college, there was a guy who firmly believed that it was a sin to have tattoos. Further, he proclaimed that it was the mark of the beast, and if you do have tattoos, you're going to hell for having them. He didn't just believe this ideology; he would preach this and blatantly tell people that they were going to hell without remorse.

So, because of my hatred toward religiosity and fundamentalism, I decided to do a fake interview with him. I pretended I was from the university's news network, and I asked him, *"What are your thoughts on tattoos and people/Christians who have them?"* He began to tell me that he believes that tattoos are a sin and people with tattoos are going to hell.

I then took off my jacket and showed him my tattoos, and told him, *"Look me in my eyes and tell me I am going to hell then."* He couldn't. Then I told him, *"If you would spend more of your time telling people about the grace, love, and mercy of Christ and exhibiting it yourself, then maybe you would have fruit, which is the evidence of our salvation. But you don't have fruit. Because you would rather use your time to solidify your judgments toward people and tell them what you think is sinful and what is not."*

This isn't my only time experiencing a religious person. I definitely have had my fair share of religious people. One time, I attended a church that looked down on a couple for going through a divorce instead of being there for them with care and love. I've had a pastor tell me that they were glad they didn't hire me at their church because I got a divorce instead of showing empathy for my situation. I've seen people kicked out of leadership and gossiped about by church people for their sin struggles. This is why friends and acquaintances of mine who are not Christians tell me that they love Jesus but hate Christianity. Because of their bad experiences with "Christians," the people I love and care for refuse to give their life to Christ, because they don't want to be a Christian.

Many of us, and I would go as far to say most of us, have experienced religious people. Maybe you've been hurt by these individuals. Maybe someone you know and love has been hurt by religious people. Maybe you attended a church or still attend a church where you were spiritually abused. Maybe you had someone who "discipled you" that would gossip to others about all of the dirt you spilled in your last discipleship meeting in the form of a "prayer request." Or maybe in your situation, it went deeper. Maybe you were physically, sexually, verbally, or psychologically abused or assaulted by a religious person.

If so, I am sorry. I mean it. I am so very sorry. If I could give you a hug, look you in the eye, and tell you that, I absolutely would, but ink on the page will have to do for now. Religious people are the cancer in the bride of Christ, and they do not represent Jesus at all.

If you've been hurt by religious people, I implore you to read the Bible. You may not want to because of your experience, but if anything, just read the gospels: Matthew, Mark, Luke, and John. Read about the actions and words of Jesus during His earthly ministry. By the time you get to the end of John chapter 21, you will notice that the actions and words of Jesus do not align with that of a religious person. A religious person's actions and words align more with a Pharisee as we see in John chapter 9.

Once you read the gospels and witness this for yourself, you will understand the second half of John chapter 9 a lot better. A man who has been healed and cleansed, now is verbally scourged and scowled by religious people and kicked out of their religion.

Jesus hears of this man being kicked out of his religion and it says that Jesus "found him." *What I have found about the grace of Jesus, is that when religious people forget you, Jesus finds you.* Jesus heard that religion got rid of this man for believing Christ is Lord, so He went out to find him to have a relationship with him.

No matter how far you have drifted off, no matter how much you want to distance yourself from the church or religion, I want to reassure you that Jesus is looking for you. Your Great Shepherd is looking for you, His beloved sheep. He wants a relationship with you, not for you to bow down to religious practice. Why do you think He healed on the sabbath? Jesus Himself didn't even bow down to empty religious ceremony, so why should we?

We close out John chapter nine with Jesus telling the blind man about spiritual blindness in front of the Pharisees. The blind man, now being able to see, understood what Jesus was teaching him because he physically was able to see after living a lifetime of blindness. The Pharisees, hearing this teaching, then ask Jesus "Are we blind?" And Jesus responds with "Yes, you are."

One time in a sermon for a youth ministry, I talked about bullies and how bullies harass people to hide the fact that they are deeply insecure, hurting, and going through an identity crisis. I then pointed out how I know for a fact there are some bullies in the room. After I got done preaching, a few students came up to me and asked me, "Am I a bully?" I told them, "I don't know you well enough to tell you whether you are a bully or not, but if you are needing to ask yourself this question, maybe you have been a bully and you were blind to it until now."

So, to you, the reader, maybe you have read through this chapter and you are asking yourself, much like the Pharisee in our text, "Am I a religious person?" I would say for you to go to the Lord with that question. I think for most Christians, we have religious parts in our heart that need to be surrendered to God. And listen, if you have been religious to people, it is okay. Jesus has grace for you. Why do you think He befriended Pharisees like Nicodemus and Joseph of Arimathea? Even the most religious people can enter into a relationship with Christ and be gracious and loving.

If after prayer, you realize that you have been religious to people rather than loving and gracious, I encourage you to apologize to those you've been religious to. And be assured, there is grace! This is why the grace of Christ is so scandalous: Even someone called a brood of vipers can be saved by the lamb of God.

If you have been hurt by a religious person or organization, before you move onto chapter nine, I want you to ask yourself these questions in a time of prayer and reflection:

1. The same grace I received from entering into a relationship with Jesus, am I showing it to those who have hurt me through their religiousness?

2. Have I forgiven the religious person or organization who hurt me?

3. What areas of my life do I find that I too am religious?

I'll see you in chapter nine!

"A Scandal → Us Death"

Key quote:

"For the wages of sin is death, but the gift of God is eternal life in Christ Jesus our Lord."
Romans 6:23

By this point, I would hope that you understand the true concept of grace better than when you first opened the pages of this book. The life and ministry of Jesus exude the truest meaning of grace to the highest degree. As we prepare to end this journey together, I want to look at the most scandalous act Jesus ever did. I had to save the best for last, right?

At the end of Jesus's life is where this specific act of grace is found, that is, the crucifixion. As Christians, we understand that we are saved from the penalty of our sin, which is death, because Jesus paid our death sentence through his death. But what if I told you that Jesus dying for our sins was only touching the surface of how scandalous this selfless act was? What if I told you that the cross of Christ means so much more than you may think?

In this chapter, I want to dive into some of the cultural, medical, biblical, and spiritual details of the crucifixion of Jesus. I want to reveal to you the full picture of what the cross of Christ means for you and me as well as talk through Jesus's final scandalous miracle.

The History of Death by Crucifixion

So, what is crucifixion? Well, it was a common, yet brutal form of execution that is believed to have been introduced by the Persians around the 4th century BCE. This form of execution was then carried on by Alexander the Great, then the Phoenicians claimed it, and finally it made its way to Rome about 300 years before Christ.

People who were crucified were executed due to very serious capital crimes and it was believed in that culture that to be crucified was the ultimate form of indecency and social indignity. Victims were hung naked on their crosses so that embarrassment would follow the victims beyond the grave. People often would be crucified for treason, murder, and political and religious agitation.

When someone was crucified, they would first be beaten and scourged severely. Then the victim would drag the crossbeam of their cross to the place of their crucifixion. When they arrived at their location, they would have nails driven into their wrists and feet. Notice, I said wrists, not hands. These nails would penetrate the medial nerve in the wrist to cause intense, radiating pain up the arm. This pain felt like a severe burning sensation that would go up the entire arm and caused the hand to go into an involuntary grip.

With the nails in the wrists and feet, those being crucified would have to pull themselves up to breathe, often dislocating their shoulders and driving splinters into their scourged flesh. When the victims would raise themselves up for a breath, the nails would rub against the damaged nerves causing each breath to be nothing less than torture.

The cross itself typically sat low, about one to two feet off of the ground so that animals could feed off of the corpses. The crucifixion victims were hung in public places, normally alongside roads. So instead of seeing a billboard, passerbys would see dead, bloody criminals getting their flesh eaten by birds and animals. This scare tactic by the Romans was their twisted way of sending a message of warning to nearby pedestrians to not commit these crimes that were committed.

With the trauma the body faced through being whipped, beaten, and losing pints of blood, crucifixion victims would mostly die by bleeding to death, dehydration, suffocation, or by having a heart attack.

Now here's the thing most people don't understand about crucifixion, these people could live and suffer on their cross for days. If they lived for too long however, the executioner would smash the legs of the victim so that they would just suffocate to death. Once deceased, victims were not buried, they were thrown into what was basically a dump for garbage and then their corpse would be eaten by animals in a hot pile of garbage.

The Biblical View of Christ Crucified

Now think about this for a moment, Jesus saw crucifixions growing up. When He would travel to Jerusalem, He most likely saw people crucified on the side of the street while He traveled. And if we believe Jesus had perfect foreknowledge, that means Jesus knew He would die like the people He passed by in His travels. Maybe knowing this truth is why Jesus got so nervous and burdened in the Garden of Gethsemane that he sweated blood while fervently praying.

Jesus would experience all the results of crucifixion as stated above (except he was not eaten by animals and didn't have his legs broken in order to fulfill prophecy). In addition, He was given a crown of thorns to go around His head. With the skin of the scalp containing more blood than any other place on the body and blood vessels being so close to the surface on the head, Jesus bled even more than the usual crucifixion victim.

Additionally, Jesus experienced pericardial and pleural effusion. Pericardial effusion is when fluid builds up around the heart, causing heart failure. Pleural effusion is when fluid builds up in the lungs and causes heart failure as well. We know this to be true because when the soldier pierced the side of Jesus, water and blood came out which is the proof that He had pericardial and pleural effusion.

Jesus got these effusions due to infection which was most likely from when He got whipped by the Romans. When this happened, the whips which had bone and metal attached to the ends, ripped out flesh from Jesus's back and implanted bacteria which would have caused infection if untreated. This means that before Jesus ever got on that cross, He was already dying.

When Jesus arrived at Calvary, He had the nails driven into his feet and wrists and then they raised His cross up and placed it into the ground. Jesus hung on that cross for six hours. From 9a.m.-3p.m. Jesus suffered and ultimately died from cardiac arrest on the cross. He hung naked with a sign above His head that said, "Jesus of Nazareth the King of the Jews" and a crown of thorns was placed firmly on His skull.

Imagine the few moments that Jesus remained on the cross after being deceased. Imagine how much of a mockery it looked like. Imagine how embarrassing and shameful it looked to be Jesus on that cross. It is not blasphemous to say that, because that was the primary goal of the Romans and the Jews who sentenced Him to death. They wanted to embarrass Jesus beyond the grave.

Not only was crucifixion a statement of ridicule and mockery, but even biblically there are spiritual consequences for someone who gets crucified.

In Deuteronomy 21:23b it states, *"...anyone who is hung on a pole is under God's curse."* Being crucified not only meant that you were tortured, killed, and embarrassed beyond the grave; it also meant that for eternity you were cursed. It was believed that to be crucified was worse than death itself because it was reserved only for those that were cursed by God.

In Galatians 3, Paul refers back to this piece of law that is found in Deuteronomy and states in verse 13, *"Christ redeemed us from the curse of the law by becoming a curse for us."* Jesus became the physical embodiment of the curse we deserved to receive, and He died so we would never be cursed or found guilty for our sin. Think about this: God came to earth to become the embodiment of your sin-curse and died to release you from that curse. Talk about grace!

Scandal #1

Now the Jews had a big issue with this idea that the Messiah was crucified. The Jews were thinking, *So you're telling me that the son of a carpenter, from Nazareth, who preached a different code than the religious leaders, and died an embarrassing and accursed death on a cross is supposed to be our Messiah?*

That's what makes this so scandalous. Most Jews to this day still do not believe that Jesus is the Messiah. I mean, how could a messiah be crucified, right?

That is the belief of the Jews. This is why Paul writes in 1 Corinthians 1:23, *"but we preach Christ crucified: a stumbling block to Jews and foolishness to Gentiles…"* A messiah, to the Jews, is someone with power, royalty, and exuded victory. Crucifixion, however, gave a message of futility, lowliness, and defeat.

Even some of the most famous philosophers during this time proclaimed that to have Christ crucified is dumb, superstitious, and pure foolishness. Both Jew and Gentile, teacher of the law and teacher of philosophy could not believe this guy named Jesus could be the Messiah.

Scandal #2

Christ's death as the Messiah was scandalous. Even more scandalous however, is Jesus's final conversation on this earth. In Luke chapter 23, Luke details for us that Jesus didn't walk the path alone to Calvary. It says that Jesus was accompanied by two other criminals who would be crucified alongside Him. When they arrived at Golgotha, Jesus, attached to His cross, was hung in the middle of the two criminals.

As the people scorned Jesus, so did these two criminals. However, one of them, called the "thief on the cross" in most traditions, stopped ridiculing Jesus and began to believe Him, and believe *in* Him.

This criminal was not a thief though. Scholars tell us that this criminal was actually a terrorist or a radical. This man was part of a rebellion against the Roman army and would randomly kill people who wouldn't join the resistance. He was a murderer, a terrorist, and most important of all, a sinner.

The criminal defended Jesus to the criminal who hung on the other side of the cross of Christ. Then he said to Jesus, "Jesus remember me when you come into your kingdom." In Greek, the word kingdom means "the royal power of the triumphant Messiah." The criminal essentially is saying to Jesus, "Jesus remember me when you take on the royal power that the triumphant Messiah obtains."

Jesus responds to this man, who up until this moment was seen as a murderer, a thief, and a terrorist, and says to him, "Truly I tell you, today you will be with me in paradise." In Greek, the word "paradise" translates to the highest regions of heaven.

A man who is moments from death after killing people through terroristic avenues, is now told from the Messiah that he will be with Jesus in the highest regions of heaven.

Scandalous Grace

Recently, I had coffee with a friend of mine who runs a ministry to help those who have been convicted of crimes and due to the severity of those crimes, they are unable to get on their feet. My friend helps these individuals start a new life so that they can move on from their past.

Many of the guys in his ministry have been convicted of sex related crimes and have been deemed by the public as "sexual predators." Because of this title, there are groups of people who try to harm or even kill these men even after they have done their time in jail and have been transformed into different people through the grace of Jesus.

These guys love Jesus. I've talked to a few of them, and they are some of the kindest men I have ever met. They made poor life decisions in their life that have affected people very negatively. But for the guys in this ministry who have given their life to Jesus, they have been pardoned of everything they have ever done according to God. In fact, there is a clean slate that has their name on it with no charges written on it that they are guilty of.

Because of their belief in Jesus, according to Jesus, they are not criminals like the world says. They are not predators like the world says. They are beloved sons of God who have been given access to the paradise of heaven.

I saved this chapter for the end of this book not just because it is Jesus's final scandalous act, it is because in order for you to answer the following questions, you need to understand what scandalous grace looks like. I have shown you through the life of Christ what that kind of grace looks like and how it is the same grace shown to you and I. It is the grace that has pardoned all of our sins we have ever done and the grace that will pardon all of the sins we will ever do in the future.

If you believe that, if you believe ANYONE can receive that grace and be excused and forgiven of ANYTHING and given a seat in heaven, I want to challenge your ceiling of grace. So here are my questions:

- Do you think those who have committed sex crimes can be redeemed and saved by the grace of Jesus?

- Do you think terrorists who have murdered through acts of hatred can be redeemed and saved by the grace of Jesus?

- If Osama Bin Laden was still alive, do you believe he could be redeemed and saved by the grace of Jesus?

- If Adolf Hitler didn't commit suicide and had someone present the gospel to him, do you believe he could be redeemed and saved by the grace of Jesus even after he ordered for six million Jews to be murdered?

- If Ted Bundy didn't receive the death penalty and someone presented the gospel to him, do you believe he could be redeemed and saved by the grace of Jesus even after he raped and murdered over thirty young women?

- If John Wayne Gayce never got executed, do you believe he could be redeemed and saved by the grace of Jesus even after he raped, strangled, and murdered thirty-three young men?

- If Jeffrey Dahmer never got murdered in jail, do you believe he could be redeemed and saved by the grace of Jesus even after he raped, killed, and dismembered seventeen men?

Well, as I mentioned a few chapters back, Jeffrey Dahmer actually did give his life to Jesus in jail and was baptized for his faith in God. And although he was murdered and ridiculed by the world for his heinous crimes, according to God, his slate was wiped clean.

If you say no to any of the questions above, you do not understand grace. Plain and simple. Jesus's last conversation on this planet was with a terrorist who murdered people and he told this man that he would be in the highest parts of heaven with Jesus because of his belief. What makes these people listed above any different?

We all are sinners. And this is why Paul writes Romans 3:23-26, so that we can grasp this concept fully. He writes:

23 for all have sinned and fall short of the glory of God, 24 and all are justified freely by his grace through the redemption that came by Christ Jesus. 25 God presented Christ as a sacrifice of atonement, through the shedding of his blood—to be received by faith. He did this to demonstrate his righteousness, because in his forbearance he had left the sins committed beforehand unpunished— 26 he did it to demonstrate his righteousness at the present time, so as to be just and the one who justifies those who have faith in Jesus.

Before moving unto our final chapter together, please ask yourself these questions:

- Do I have grace with all people, or do I show grace to people who only minorly sin?

- Do I have grace for all sins, or just the ones I don't think are that bad?

- Do I judge people because of their past sins?

- Do I keep a record of wrongs, or do people have a blank slate with me?

I'll see you in our final chapter.

CHAPTER TEN

"Conclusion"

Key quote:

"For the grace of God has appeared that offers salvation to all people. It teaches us to say "No" to ungodliness and worldly passions, and to live self-controlled, upright and godly lives in this present age..."

Titus 2:11-12

As we close out our time together, I want to say thank you for your effort and taking on the challenge of reading this book with an open heart and mind. As I have been writing these words, I have been praying for you to experience the grace of Christ in a new and fresh way.

Writing this book has been a blessing to me personally. When I was writing, I noticed that as I wrote on grace, the more my ceiling of grace was challenged, and I hope the same happened for you.

In fact, as I was writing this book, I went through a time in my life when I wasn't showing grace to some people who were doing wrong to me. I was frustrated, I was speaking ill of them, and I found myself beginning to gossip about these people.

Then, one day, I confided in a pastor friend of mine and he told me after I was done ranting and raving, "For someone writing a book about grace, you don't have much grace for others." That wasn't easy to hear, but I needed to hear it. I needed to learn how to live a life that overflowed with grace. This didn't mean that I was allowing people to step all over me, but rather, it was me learning how to love people with a love so strong that I could forgive others regardless of what they did to me.

I would be doing you a disservice if I wrote this entire book and I didn't talk through the next step, the step I had to learn in the process of writing this book: How to live a grace-filled life. How do we live a life that exudes the very grace we have been shown by Christ? How do we walk out grace in our relationships with others?

A Grace Filled Life

When Jesus was asked what the number one law was, he responded in Mark 12:30-31, *"Love the Lord your God with all your heart and with all your soul and with all your mind and with all your strength.' The second is this: 'Love your neighbor as yourself.' There is no commandment greater than these."*

The two greatest things we can ever do in this life is to love God above everything and to love our neighbor. Many of us will say that we do this, but when it comes to loving our neighbor, I believe many of us fall short in this category.

The Greek word for "love" in this scripture is not *phileo* which is brotherly love. This word typically would be used for interpersonal love that wasn't a romantic type of love. Instead, the word used here interestingly enough is the word *agape* which is used as the word describing God's love for us. If I were to define what agape love is, it can be defined as "To love in spite of _____." This is where grace comes into play.

To love God fully, we must love our neighbor as well. In each of these chapters, I talked a lot to those who have experienced hurt and pain at the hand of someone else. Let me ask you, do you forgive them? Forgiveness and grace go hand in hand, you cannot have one without the other. They are of equal importance and Jesus believes that too.

In the gospels, Jesus speaks on forgiveness often. He says:

- Matthew 18:21-22 *"Lord, how often should I forgive someone who sins against me? Seven times?" "No, not seven times," Jesus says, "but seventy times seven!"*

- Matthew 6:12 *"Forgive us our sins, as we have forgiven those who sin against us."*

- Luke 17:3-4 *"If another believer sins, rebuke that person; then if there is repentance, forgive. Even if that person wrongs you seven times a day and each time turns again and asks forgiveness, you must forgive."*

- Mark 11:25 *"When you are praying, first forgive anyone you are holding a grudge against, so that your Father in heaven will forgive your sins, too."*

So, what happens if we don't forgive? Well, Jesus says in Matthew 6:14-15 *"For if you forgive other people when they sin against you, your heavenly Father will also forgive you. But if you do not forgive others their sins, your Father will not forgive your sins."* If you don't forgive, you will not be forgiven. If you are not forgiven, you are not pardoned. And if you aren't pardoned, do you receive grace? I'll let you answer that one.

So, how do we live a grace filled life? Well, to live a life like that we need to forgive those who have done us wrong. It is more than just a prayer to God saying, "God, I forgive them." Whoever it is that did you wrong, give them a call, shoot them a text, don't gaslight them, just tell them what they did and that you truly forgive them and pardon them for everything they ever have done to you.

Now you could say to me, "Well you don't know what they did to me." And that is a normal human response when talking through the concept of forgiveness. But what I would say as a response to that is, "Regardless of what they did to you, what are you going to do about it?"

I heard someone say one time that forgiveness is like taking poison but expecting the other person to die. Did you realize that unforgiveness is your personal problem? I understand maybe you experienced something super traumatic or hurtful at the hand of someone else, and I am sorry you had that experience, but I love you enough to tell you that choosing not to forgive someone is your problem, no one else's.

I'll never forget one time when someone came and told me that they had been raped at a young age. My heart was broken, and my jaw dropped wide open in shock and disbelief. I couldn't fathom what I was hearing because what happened to this person was so terrible.

They proceeded to tell me that they had so much hatred toward the person that did that to them, and they wanted them to rot in jail and die there. I sat there and listened to this person and when they were done, I said to them, "Even if they got thrown in jail, even if they did suffer, and even if they were killed, at the end of it, you wouldn't feel any better. You would still hold onto that unforgiveness and never be freed from those shackles. I am sorry for what happened to you, but you need to choose to forgive them or else it will stay with you your entire life and you'll never be able to move on with your life."

Even to the cross, Jesus prayed for God to forgive those that mocked Him and nailed Him to the very cross he was dying on. It is a harsh reality, but if you do not have forgiveness for people, you cannot experience the grace of Christ. But when you choose forgiveness, you can accept grace and when you accept grace, you can live a grace-filled life.

My Final Story to You

When I was in high school, there was a guy who was in many of my classes, and he hated God. He didn't just hate God, he mocked God and anyone who believed in Him. Now I didn't get saved until I was in college, but I had believed in God since I was young. I would go to church, I would read my Bible, and I upheld my purity.

Every day I brought my Bible to school, wore a purity ring, and people often asked me questions about God because I was the closest thing to a Christian that they knew. Well, this guy would antagonize me because of my values and my belief in God. Many times, he would hide my Bible, rip pages out of my Bible, put things in my Bible, or even spit in my Bible. He would go home and research Bible verses that, out of context, sound inappropriate and would ask me in front of a bunch of people why that was in the Bible. Additionally, one time he knew where in the

Bible the story of the crucifixion was and had me read it to him. When I got to the part where Jesus died, he would laugh in my face and yell at me, "HA HA! YOUR GOD IS DEAD!" This guy was just super antagonistic.

Two years out of high school, I was in my car and that guy randomly came up in my thoughts and for some reason I felt like I needed to call him. I had him as a friend on Facebook, so I called him on that app and guess what, he picked up.

He talked to me in a very somber tone and went on to tell me that it's super weird I was calling because he was about to commit suicide. In that moment I chose forgiveness towards him and because of that forgiveness, it opened up his heart to be willing to listen to my counsel.

By the end of the conversation, he dropped his plans to kill himself and entered into a relationship with Jesus. The very guy who never let me hear the end of his abrasive comments about God and Christianity gave his life to that very God and entered into a twelve-week discipleship program with me.

If I had not shown forgiveness, I would not have been able to be used by God to show the grace of Christ to this guy. If you want to live a life overflowing with the scandalous grace of Jesus, you must first forgive.

So, to end our time together, I have three questions for you to reflect on:

Who is someone who has done wrong to me?

Have I truly forgiven them in my heart or just with my lips?

What can I do to show to this person that I have truly forgiven them for what they've done?

Once you've done this. You can feel free to close the book and live your life with scandalous grace. Thank you for your time, your attention, and your willingness to learn about the scandalous grace of Jesus, how it applies to us, and how we can apply it to others.

Bibliography

"1 Corinthians 1:23." *The Bible: New International Version.* London: NIV, 2008.

"1 Corinthians 15:33." *The Bible: New International Version.* London: NIV, 2008.

"1 Timothy 1:15-16." *The Bible: New King James Version.* Nashville: Thomas Nelson, 2015.

"2 Corinthians 5:21." *Holy Bible: English Standard Version.* Wheaton, IL: Crossway Bibles, 2001.

"2 Corinthians 12:9." *The Bible: New International Version.* London: NIV, 2008.

"Acts 1:8 NLT." *Holy Bible New Living Translation.* Wheaton, IL: Tyndale House Publishers, Inc, 2004.

"Blue Letter Bible." *Blue Letter Bible.* https://www. blueletterbible.org/.

"Deuteronomy 21:23." *The Bible: New International Version.* London: NIV, 2008.

"Deuteronomy 22:20-21." *The Bible: New International Version.* London: NIV, 2008.

"Exodus 35:2." *The Bible: New International Version.* London: NIV, 2008.

"Galatians 3:13." *The Bible: New International Version.* London: NIV, 2008.

Hall, John Mark. "Casting Crowns Who Am I Lyrics."

AZLyrics.com. https://www.azlyrics.com/lyrics/ castingcrowns/whoami.html.

"Hebrews 4:16." *Holy Bible New Living Translation.* Wheaton, IL: Tyndale House Publishers, Inc, 2004.

"Isaiah 12:3." *The Bible: New International Version.* London: NIV, 2008.

"Isaiah 38:16-17." *The Bible: New International Version.* London: NIV, 2008.

"Isaiah 64:8." *The Bible: New International Version.* London: NIV, 2008.

"John 3:3." *The Bible: New International Version.* London: NIV, 2008.

"John 3:4." *The Bible: New International Version.* London: NIV, 2008.

"John 8:5." *The Bible: New International Version.* London: NIV, 2008.

"John 8:7." *The Bible: New International Version.* London: NIV, 2008.

"John 8:9." *The Bible: New International Version.* London: NIV, 2008.

"John 8:11." *The Bible: New International Version.* London: NIV, 2008.

"John 9:5." *The Bible: New International Version.* London: NIV, 2008.

"John 9:11." *Holy Bible: English Standard Version.*

Wheaton, IL: Crossway Bibles, 2001.

"John 15:13-15." *The Bible: New International Version.* London: NIV, 2008.

"John 16:24." *The Bible: New International Version.* London: NIV, 2008.

"Leviticus 13:45-46." *Holy Bible New Living Translation.* Wheaton, IL: Tyndale House Publishers, Inc, 2004.

"Luke 1:34." *The Bible: New International Version.* London: NIV, 2008.

"Luke 5:30." *The Bible: New International Version.* London: NIV, 2008.

"Luke 17:3-4." *Holy Bible New Living Translation.* Wheaton, IL: Tyndale House Publishers, Inc, 2004.

"Mark 11:25." *Holy Bible New Living Translation.* Wheaton, IL: Tyndale House Publishers, Inc, 2004.

"Mark 12:30-31." *The Bible: New International Version.* London: NIV, 2008.

"Matthew 5:17." *The Bible: New International Version.* London: NIV, 2008.

"Matthew 6:12." *Holy Bible New Living Translation.* Wheaton, IL: Tyndale House Publishers, Inc, 2004.

"Matthew 6:14-15." *The Bible: New International Version.* London: NIV, 2008.

"Matthew 9:12-13." *The Bible: New International*

Version. London: NIV, 2008.

"Matthew 11:28." *The Bible: New International Version*. London: NIV, 2008.

"Matthew 18:21-22." *Holy Bible New Living Translation*. Wheaton, IL: Tyndale House Publishers, Inc, 2004.

Neusner, Jacob. "Shabbat 108:20." *The Mishnah*. Atlanta, GA: Scholars Press, 1993.

Pilgrim, David. "What Was Jim Crow." Ferris State University, 2000. https://www.ferris.edu/HTMLS/news/jimcrow/what.htm.

"Psalms 23:5." *The Bible: New International Version*. London: NIV, 2008.

"Psalms 118:8-9." *The Bible: New International Version*. London: NIV, 2008.

"Romans 3:23-26." *The Bible: New International Version*. London: NIV, 2008.

"Romans 6:14." *The Bible: New International Version*. London: NIV, 2008.

"Romans 6:23." *The Bible: New International Version*. London: NIV, 2008.

"Romans 8:38-39." *The Bible: New International Version*. London: NIV, 2008.

"Titus 2:11-12." *The Bible: New International Version*. London: NIV, 2008.

About the Author

Billy Mossberg is a Student Pastor in Orlando, Florida. Billy grew up in Lisbon, Connecticut, and moved to Florida in 2014 to attend Southeastern University where he graduated with a bachelor of science in Practical Ministries. He is married to his wife, Jadxia, and they serve alongside one another at their church, Discovery Church.